About the Author

Ron Falconer was born and raised in a small village in the highlands of Scotland. He was educated at Tain Royal Academy, spent some years with the Royal Air Force and formed his own business as an architectural draughtsman. Always a dreamer and curious traveller, he built his own boat, *Fleur d'Ecosse*, as a means of transport and sailed away to the life of a wandering nomad. For twelve years he travelled more than 50 000 miles around the world, visiting over 100 ports and experiencing many cultures. Finally he took his new wife and young family to live alone on a deserted island. He now lives quietly on the island of Moorea, close to Tahiti.

Together Alone

RON FALCONER

BANTAM BOOKS
SYDNEY • AUCKLAND • NEW YORK • LONDON

TOGETHER ALONE
A BANTAM BOOK

First published in Australia and New Zealand in 2004
by Bantam

National Library of Australia
Cataloguing-in-Publication Entry

Falconer, Ron.
Together alone.

ISBN 1 86325 428 5.

1. Falconer, Ron – Travel. 2. Survival skills – Kiribati – Millennium Island.
3. Millennium Island (Kiribati) – Social life and customs. 4. Kiribati –
Politics and government. I. Title.

919.68104

Transworld Publishers,
a division of Random House Australia Pty Ltd
20 Alfred Street, Milsons Point, NSW 2061
http://www.randomhouse.com.au

Random House New Zealand Limited
18 Poland Road, Glenfield, Auckland

Transworld Publishers,
a division of The Random House Group Ltd
61-63 Uxbridge Road, London W5 5SA

Random House Inc
1745 Broadway, New York, New York 10036

Cover Design by Darian Causby/Highway 51
Typeset by Midland Typesetters, Maryborough, Victoria
Printed and bound by Griffin Press, Netley, South Australia

10 9 8 7 6 5 4 3 2 1

For Anne, Alexandre and Anaïs

Author's Note

The birth of this book evoked some deep emotions. I really wanted to forget the whole story – too many sensitive nerve ends still remained exposed to be able to look back without acute pain. Then the very idea of trying to capture in words what had been a full, passionate and profound experience seemed an impossible task. So much had happened – physical, emotional, spiritual and philosophical.

With much trepidation I began. With endless patience and determination I accumulated a large stack of rough pencil-written pages. Pleased with my mammoth achievement, I took my manuscript to a journalist friend. He just shook his head politely at my disjointed and messy presentation. But I was learning. With time, and aided by a marvellous little typewriter/word processor, I cleaned up my jumble of thoughts, faced emotions and established facts. The story staggered on through the years to slowly evolve to its present form. It may be interesting to note that it has taken twice the time of the adventure to recreate the story in words.

Ron Falconer
Moorea

The most beautiful and profound emotion we can experience is the sensation of the mystical. It is the sower of all
true science. He to whom this emotion is a stranger, who
can no longer wonder and stand rapt in awe, is as good as
dead. To know that what is impenetrable to us really exists,
manifesting itself as the highest wisdom and the most
radiant beauty, which our dull faculties can comprehend
only in their primitive forms, this knowledge, this feeling is
at the centre of true religiousness.

Albert Einstein

Contents

PART THREE   LETTING GO

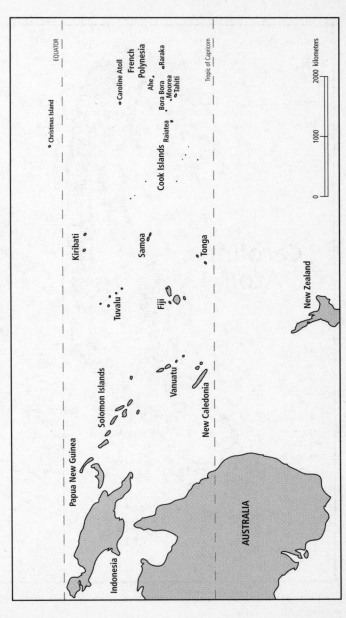

South Pacific Ocean

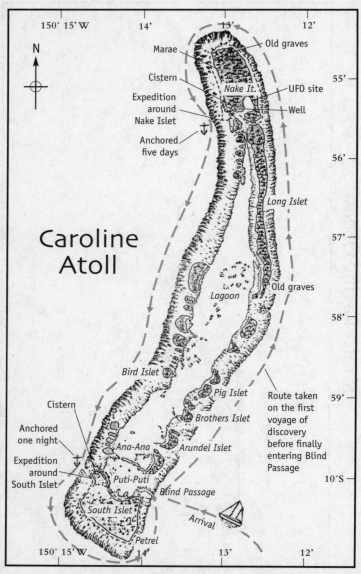

Caroline Atoll; route taken on the first voyage of discovery, before entering Blind Passage.

Foreword

Very little was known about Caroline Atoll when our small biological expedition arrived at this tropical paradise. It was in need of a scientific survey before its nomination as a World Heritage site could be submitted to the United Nations.

'Caroline Atoll is uninhabited,' we had been told by the owners of the island, the Kiribati Government – which made the presence of the Falconer family quite surprising. We saw them as a modern-day Swiss Family Robinson.

We were pleased to find Ron, Anne, Alexandre and Anaïs acting as competent caretakers of this perfect little place. The Falconers were eating locally grown produce and catching fish whenever possible. They used whatever was washed up on the beach in ways that boggled the mind, and held us in rapt admiration of such true ingenuity at work. They had developed a pragmatic blend of Polynesian and Western ways, and they amazed us with their determination to overcome outside influences that threatened to over-whelm their self-made paradise.

Ron Falconer is quite a character – adventurous yet relaxed, private, yet a talented singer and musician. His abilities as a gifted storyteller have served him well in the pages of this book. If you are looking for 'tried and true' desert island survival skills, or a classic family adventure story, then read on, you will not be disappointed!

Dr Graham Wragg (R/V Te Manu)
University of Oxford
January 2002

PART ONE

Arrival

Caroline Atoll: The Dream Becomes Real

We're sailing north from Tahiti toward the equator. Overhead the tropical sun is hot – even the moderate easterly trade wind feels warm on my bare skin. Small, puffy white clouds drift slowly by in an otherwise clear blue sky. Sailing aboard *Fleur d'Ecosse* is as comfortable and reassuring as being in a mother's womb.

I lie in the cockpit with my head propped up on a pillow, occasionally moving my book aside to glance at the compass course. We sail along peacefully, a white apparition in the centre of a lonely circle of ocean that is far from land and the regular shipping lanes. From time to time I sit up to scan the horizon for any sign of thunderclouds that could bring on a squall and disturb our peace. Sometimes I remain upright long enough to watch the windvane automatically control the rudder and bring the boat back on course; then I go back to my book. It's hard to pay attention to my reading, however. I'm not as calm as my relaxed position would suggest. This voyage is the first step toward fulfilment of a long-held dream.

Anne rests below, trying to catch up on sleep since she has been fully occupied with the demands of our two young children. Anaïs, soon to be two years old, is taking a nap. She has suffered some seasickness and remains a little lethargic. Alexandre, two years older than his sister, stays quiet and busy on the floor of the cabin, arranging his favourite plastic bricks into pirate ships and fantasy castles. Dou-Dou, the cat, lies curled up in her usual snug place on the main bunk while Kiki, our short-legged mongrel, remains spread out and inert on the cool floor. The two parakeets, Kwili and Raki, are the liveliest aboard. They chatter and bob around in their cage, scattering the husks of their sunflower seeds all over the chart table.

We are nomads, sea nomads – complete, like Noah, with our own handmade boat and menagerie of animals. Our destiny is a very special island that lies right in the centre of the Pacific Ocean. We feel we are being blown along toward our future by the winds of fate, since so many events, some planned and others strangely coincidental, have brought us to this point.

Now, after five calm days sailing northward, we are close to our destination: Caroline Atoll, which would later be known as Millennium Island, the first place on earth to witness the dawning of the year 2000.

I check my navigation fixes. From the morning star sights, I estimate the distance still to run. 'We're about twelve miles away,' I call to Anne. 'We should see it any minute.'

Anne, instantly alert, bounds up on deck and begins to search the horizon. An intense person who can put con-centration and energy into anything she chooses, she is enthusiastic about the boat, always ready to change sails and complete the navigation. She has been my skilled and faithful mate (in both senses of the word) for several years. But I know she's not one hundred per cent in favour of this adventure. She's following my dream with me, which I realise is not quite the same as following a dream she designed for herself. In addition, she's anxious about the children, who will be living so far from medical assistance. While I share her anxiety to some extent, my excitement at the moment obliterates all negativity.

Suddenly she cries out, 'I can see it!' She points. 'There, there, look!'

Together we watch as a thin smudgy outline appears from time to time between the undulating swells. Although it's hot on deck and we're both tired, for a moment our discomfort is forgotten and we share the thrill and satisfaction of having found our landfall – this island that could possibly be our new home. The series of navigational dots and crosses we've been following faithfully now become redundant. We can see the actual island, and we head directly for it.

Slowly the low grey outline rises up out of the sea and separates into small, green, tree-covered islets. A thin white sandy beach that underscores the islets appears behind the breaking white surf. The coral barrier reef is flat and wide. My eyes scour this solid image. Once only the product of an active imagination, the abstract dream has materialised into reality. This is the point to which everything in my life of wandering and searching has been heading: a completely uninhabited island on which to probe the fundamentals of life.

'It looks desolate,' Anne remarks.

'Well, it's uninhabited and isolated,' I reply a little defensively. I want her to share my eagerness. Alexandre and Kiki make their way to the back door of the cockpit and hang out the door together. Kiki sniffs the air while Alexandre gazes quietly shoreward.

'And me!' Anaïs demands urgently from her cushions on the cockpit floor. She clings on tightly as I lift her high. When her head comes clear of the hatch, she squeals 'Oooouuu' in surprise at the nearness of land.

Through the fine mist of sea spray blown inland from the breaking waves, the line of islets that stretch away to the north gives the impression of an exotic and mysterious wonderland. Close in to the reef the boat rolls and pitches in the short, choppy seas created by the backwash of the waves. We hold on tight and search along the breakers for the entrance to what on the chart is called, somewhat ominously, 'Blind Passage'.

We see no sign of any obvious pass. Just as I'm giving up hope, a narrow blue gap appears in the long line of white foam – an opening in the reef. It must be Blind Passage. For a while I watch this supposed entrance, which looks tiny. On both sides of it, waves build up to breaking point, then tumble and thunder ashore.

One of the reasons this island has remained uninhabited and undeveloped is the total lack of shallow water around it. From the steep edge of the coral, the water plunges almost vertically to the ocean floor far below. There is no place to anchor safely, so if we are to settle on Caroline Atoll, we have to be able to enter this small passage. Unfortunately it lies on the dangerous, windward side of the island.

I circle around in front of the entrance, where I can see a strong current flowing out. This outgoing current creates a series of steep, high, rolling waves as it encounters the opposing force of the open sea. Behind the opening it's possible to see clearly the small pass that runs in across the reef. There it waits, as calm and serene as a mythical mermaid who tempts all sailors to enter her world and enjoy her pleasures.

A small group of large dolphins – the porpoises, not the fish – suddenly appears. 'Look, we're getting a warm welcome!' I shout to Anne. At least for a moment we're distracted from the serious problem of the pass. The dolphins crisscross in front of the bow and play games in the turbulent current. As they turn their heads to look up for an instant at Anne on the foredeck, I can hear the plaintive peep-peep of their calling voices. For quite a few minutes we are mesmerised, like tourists entertained by the locals on a visit to a friendly Polynesian island. The children happily call back to them.

The opening, although small and dangerous, looks passable, or so I want to believe. But the current coming out presents a significant problem. It could hold us back at the worst possible moment, that is, close in to the breakers and solid reef but still outside in the turbulent seas. Since I've been lulled by thoughts of a calm place to rest, and welcomed by the friendly dolphins, my tired mind has to struggle to face the hard truth. Reluctantly I have to accept that this is not the moment to try to enter Blind Passage. To compensate for my disappointment I philosophise that Caroline, this maiden of the South Seas, has begun to show some of her coy feminine characteristics.

I start up the diesel motor. We head north along the east coast, staying close to the fringing reef. Since Kiki hates the motor, she hides in the corner farthest away from the thumping monster. Anaïs is the opposite and is quickly lulled to sleep by the vibrations. The parakeets as usual make the most disturbance, with a continual competitive chatter that won't stop until the offensive motor is finally silenced.

Alexandre stays in the cockpit, carefully watching the shore. We have another mission on this voyage: we're searching for a lost yachtsman. And if he is here, Alexandre wants to be the one to find him. 'Look for a flag, a fire or bits from a shipwreck,' I tell him to add fuel to his enthusiasm.

'Maybe he's already dead,' he suggests flatly. Nevertheless he continues to give the shore his full attention.

Caroline Atoll, like most of her sisters in the Pacific

Ocean, is a ring-shaped live coral reef composed of several islets. A coral atoll is formed when an underwater volcano erodes and sinks after becoming dormant. The hollow area that forms in the centre becomes a lagoon. Usually there is a pass through the coral ring, a clear deep-water opening into the lagoon created and kept open by the daily tides that rush in and out. This natural opening provides an entry for boats. However, sometimes, as on Caroline, the barrier reef closes off this entry and all that's left is a long crack in the coral that runs across the barrier reef but peters out into a blind alley before entering the lagoon.

The total land area of Caroline is only about one and a half square miles, and this small land area is further divided among thirty-nine islets. We continue to move past some of them.

Anne, on deck, wears her protective sun gear, an anti-sun-worshipper's official uniform: full-length white cotton trousers and a long-sleeved white cotton shirt. All the material for our clothes comes from one source: flour sacks bought cheaply from a bakery. Her eyes are protected by ski-type sunglasses and on her head she wears a hat that she wove herself from the long fronds of the coconut leaf. She's watching for any isolated coral heads, leaning her compact, white-clad body forward into the pulpit. Staring ahead in total and serious concentration, she looks like a combination of Joan of Arc in full battle charge and one of those figureheads of angelic innocence which used to grace old sailing ships. It makes me happy to look at her.

Anne and I have been travelling together for five years now, but it was seven years ago that I first met her on the island of Sark in the Channel Islands. I was visiting the island and had left *Fleur d'Ecosse* safely secured in the small harbour. Enjoying a meditative midday beer alone in the Mermaid Pub, I glimpsed, from the back, a young woman striding confidently across the floor. Alone, she made her way directly to the other side of the room where, without ordering a drink, she settled in a corner to read a book. I took time to study her. There was something strong and rebellious about her style that immediately aroused my interest. She wore her hair and clothes long and loose in gypsy fashion. Her face was round and pleasing, with what seemed to be a permanent enigmatic smile that was shy but tense.

For a while I returned to my own preoccupation: the business of sorting out a head full of new experiences. I had just completed a circumnavigation of our planet, which had involved four years of constant travelling and sailing, the solitude broken by the occasional, vagrant emotional involvement. Now I had to concentrate on the direction of my future. In principle I was heading home to my native Scotland, but my ultimate destination, I suspected, lay somewhere back in the South Pacific where I had lost my heart to the tropical island lifestyle.

My eyes returned to the far corner where the woman remained absorbed in her book. After about an hour she moved back across the room. As she passed close to the bar, I made a polite effort to catch her eye. I failed. She disappeared outside.

Later that same day I ran into her again in the Belle View, the second of a total of three pubs on the island of Sark. Now she was part of a group sharing a large table. I sat down directly opposite her and, in my strolling minstrel manner, brought out my autoharp and began to serenade her with romantic ballads in my somewhat ragged Scottish style. She appeared to be totally indifferent, unimpressed by either my repertoire or my physical presence. It took much tactful and persistent coaxing, aided perhaps by the free-flowing alcohol, for me to find out that she was a 23-year-old French mathematics teacher named Anne Christophe. She had her own tent and was staying at the local campsite.

When we all finally left the pub, long after the official closing time, the night was warm, the sky clear and starry. I gently took her hand. Just as gently, she pulled it away. As a last gesture, I invited her to visit my boat in the cool light of the following day.

I was more than a little surprised when she turned up next morning on the quay. Alas, she was leaving, and had just come to say goodbye before returning to France. We spent a pleasant hour on board discussing English words in a Thomas Hardy novel she was studying. Then we exchanged addresses, promising to stay in touch. Once more she disappeared, leaving me with the strong sensation of something begun and not finished.

I sailed home and settled in Scotland for two years. Yet I wasn't really settled at all. I was still living on *Fleur d'Ecosse*, since I had let my house prior to my round-the-world trip. Now, since my wayward spirit still longed for movement, more adventure, and something else that I was just in the process of defining, I sold the house and deposited the money in a tax-free bank account.

This money was my nest egg, strictly for 'emergencies only,' such as a serious medical situation or airline tickets back to Scotland in the event of total loss of the boat. My month-to-month expenses, which would now be confined to basic food supplies like brown rice, flour, canned milk and butter, a little diesel fuel for the motor and kerosene for the cooking stove, would come from my small but regular military pension. This was compensation for an injury during a tour of active service with the RAF in Cyprus, which left me without two of the fingers on my left hand.

I was by no means rich. What I had was a precious system of freedom to travel where and when I pleased. My plan was to return to the Pacific islands, and ultimately to live on an isolated and uninhabited desert island. But not alone – I wasn't that much of a loner. Lately my 'family unit' had consisted of me and my faithful boat, and since that now seemed incomplete, I envisioned enriching that unit to include a woman. My thoughts turned to Anne. To my surprise, I received a postcard from her.

I sailed away again, down the west coast of Scotland and England, to arrive eventually in France. I carried with me Anne's postcard, on which she had written 'What are you doing these days?' She was about to find out.

When I arrived at her flat she was not at home, so I waited outside her front door until she showed up. Now it was her turn to be surprised, as I had been the day she came to visit me on my boat on Sark.

It wasn't an easy romance. Anne had strong, independent tendencies, which I liked, except that her fiery resistance to any hint of male domination caused some friction between us. She appeared to delight in being against rather than for anything. Still, we were definitely attracted to each other and we shared a personal and practical seriousness as well as a general distaste for the current political and social system.

We met a few times but didn't appear to be going anywhere. I took a break from my wooing and went walkabout for a couple of weeks. When I returned she was more relaxed and friendly, and she invited me to stay in her flat. We went for walks, held hands, and drank a little wine together, but we slept in separate bedrooms. Finally one night, as we both lay awake and restless, she called through from her room, 'I suppose you'd better come to bed.' She was intense, quiet, and passionate in her lovemaking.

Three weeks later, while treating ourselves to a pizza, a carafe of red wine empty on our table, I asked her to come and live on a desert island with me. At first she laughed, not at all sure I was serious. When I assured her I was quite serious, she asked the natural question, 'Why would you want to live on a desert island?'

Why indeed? Why would any normal person choose to leave normal society and embrace isolation? I tried to explain: 'It's a dual adventure for me. First there's the physical challenge of surviving on my own – on *our* own – as close to nature as possible and without the help of all those things we think we need.

'And second, there's the inner journey, which I've already begun while sailing around the world. Organised society is so complicated that it's hard to tell what's natural and what's just a matter of our training. I have this idea that if I can get away and examine everything without these distractions, I can de-program myself, clear out the bullshit. Instead of playing a game, I want to reach the purity of being a human animal, partly by being close to other animals. Getting into their minds, in a way.'

As I took a deep breath, gathering my thoughts in order to continue my lofty explanation, Anne queried, 'What gives you the arrogance to think you can discover something new, something the great philosophers haven't already come up with?' That stopped me for the moment. But I noticed she was intrigued – I'd reactivated the basic rebel in her. I had also been tempting her with visions of the beauty and ease of living in Polynesia.

At this point, however, she had a lot more to give up than I did. She had her teaching job, her flat, and friends and family to think about. It was only after spending more time together, including a trial sail during her Easter holidays, that our futures began to slide together. Since I'd seen her handle the sailing so well, practically taking over all the navigation, I knew she'd be a good crew. She liked the boat and the idea of travelling.

Finally she said she was prepared to give it a try, but on

one condition: if she came along, she wanted children. Children! I hadn't thought about expanding the family unit that far. On the other hand, if we could handle it, children would add a rich dimension to our proposed adventure. I agreed. Nobody mentioned marriage; our agreement was a bigger commitment than most marriages. (In fact, we did eventually get married, but not until later in our voyage.)

Despite some lingering reservations, Anne bravely gave up her job and rented flat to move aboard. She brought along with her a pressure cooker, a hand coffee grinder, her cat, and around fifty books. She told her parents only that we were going down to Portugal.

Well, we've come a long way from Portugal, geographically as well as psychologically. Now we've arrived at this deserted island – our potential home – which lies just ahead. If only we can land here.

2

Sharks and Other Perils

I'm beside myself with eagerness to explore this lonely atoll, even if we can't land the boat. Maybe I can find a place where we can pull in close enough to drop anchor and approach in the inflatable dinghy. I return to my navigation and spread out Caroline's chart in the cockpit. I read off each islet as we pass by on our way north.

Arundel Islet: I know that a man named Arundel was the prime mover of the old settlement that existed here one hundred years ago. He also drew up the Admiralty chart I'm using. Next comes Brother's Islet: a fairly common name in Tahiti. If Pig Islet took its name from the animals, there is certainly no sign of any now. Long Islet is the old graveyard. Finally, Nake Islet: Tahitian for North Islet. Each islet is a mass of greenery with low bushes around the outer edges that protect the larger trees in the middle. A few high coconut trees pop their mop-like heads clear through the rest of the foliage. Frigate birds rest almost stationary over the trees and comfortably ride the constant rising trade wind. A large dark cloud made up of thousands of terns circles over the lagoon.

We continue north, passing mile after mile of bare, clean beach. We note only a rusted 45-gallon drum and a very large straight log. Alexandre is disappointed. He had his mind set on finding a wild marooned yachtsman on the beach, or at the very least a good shipwreck.

We sail around the top of the atoll into the blissfully calm sea on the west coast of Nake Islet. At once we are sheltered from the fresh easterly wind. A soft offshore breeze carries with it the familiar hot musty coral island smells: dead coconut leaves, damp sand, bird droppings and the unique mouldy smell of the coral itself.

We're so tired after our five-day voyage from Tahiti that we want only to rest. We search hard for a place shallow enough to anchor in, but find only deep water. In desperation we move closer and closer in to the reef itself. Now I see there are big swells running in towards the reef, possibly from a storm or cyclone hundreds of miles away to our west. We rise and fall with these large surges as they pass under the boat. When they suddenly make landfall, they rise up to a great height and crash forward onto the reef in a huge mass of tumbling, rolling water. A deep trough follows, and a momentary grand waterfall from the backwash falls vertically, foaming back over the now exposed high steep edge of the reef.

Carefully I watch the electronic depth sounder as we move cautiously in towards this scene of wild action. It purrs quietly, but shows no bottom. On deck Anne desperately searches for any change of colour in the water, indicating a shallow area. She finds nothing. We continue in toward the reef, closer, closer still, until the taste of the salt spray from the breakers is strong in my dry mouth. Just as I'm ready to back away, a reading on the sounder shows up: thirty feet to the bottom. The anchor is ready at Anne's feet. All her attention is focused on the breakers ahead.

'Okay, Okay!' I scream over the roar of the surf. 'Now! Let it go, now!' With the engine in full reverse, we slowly move away. I watch Anne let out the chain, then the nylon warp. I hesitate as she ties on a buoy to float the warp away from the sharp coral below. More warp, another buoy, then more warp still until we lie some distance clear of the reef. Meticulously Anne completes her final figure-eight attachment to the cleat.

For the moment the steady trade wind holds us away from the reef. We lower another anchor over the stern. It goes down, down, and down. We let out the full two hundred and fifty feet of warp without finding bottom. The anchor rests in vertical suspension. It's the best we can do. If we drift toward the reef, hopefully this stern anchor will hook up on something before we're swept in by the waves and battered against the reef.

Although calm at the moment, our situation remains precarious. The regular swells soothe us a little as we settle to their false but comforting rhythm. The sounds of the seabirds occasionally penetrate the constant pounding roar of the nearby surf. We have arrived. We take time out to organise the boat, then enjoy the sunset. We gaze in towards this mysterious island as the green colours ashore fade against the darkening sky. The half-moon brightens in the sky overhead only to highlight the menacing line of foaming breakers.

Anne settles the children in bed, then returns to the cockpit. Tired and anxious, we share a prolonged and reassuring hug in the relative calm of the soft moonlit evening. Then she retires to her bed. Alone in the cockpit with the sensation of her body still warm on my skin, I face the long night watch ahead. The night slides by in a series of restless catnaps, interrupted repeatedly as I am jolted awake by the nightmarish feelings that we are being swept to disaster on the deadly reef.

In the morning, even though the surf is dangerously high, I prepare the inflatable and don my anti-sun clothing and plastic sandals to prevent my feet being lacerated by the sharp coral. The main difficulty of doing anything outdoors ten degrees south of the equator is the heat of the blazing sun. Not only does it sap energy, but half an hour's exposure will severely burn any exposed skin. Fully prepared for the elements, I lay my machete on the floor of the dinghy and push off.

This is my first attempt ever to land on a barrier reef by surfing ashore. My lack of confidence is not helped by the impression that the breakers are becoming bigger and bigger as I get closer, while the dinghy seems to get smaller. I rise and fall with the regular rhythm of the swells as I wait just behind the breakers. Tensely I study their pattern as they pass under me. First they grow larger and larger, then recede a little.

During a brief recession I take my chance and begin rowing furiously towards the shore. The next breaking swell picks up the dinghy in its course. I struggle to keep control and avoid being capsized as I am driven fast ahead into the tumbling surf. The solid reef appears under me. I jump out and can feel my heart pumping as I run through the rush of now outgoing water. I pull the dinghy behind and away from the threatening waterfall that wants to drag me back into its grasp.

Suddenly a black-tipped reef shark flashes in toward my feet. Uh-oh, I hadn't planned on that. Then I remember that my guidebook said that these reef sharks are timid. In fact, the shark disappears, and I relax. A goonish grin spreads slowly across my face and my body tingles in excitement as my feet absorb the sensations and touch of this special island. I wave to Alexandre and Anne in the cockpit before turning away from the terror of the surf and in toward the shore. Close to the trees it's hot, calm and silent. The smell of coral is strong. I lift the dinghy, putting it high up the clean coral beach. I feel as if I've just landed on the moon. I should have brought a suitable flag to mark the occasion.

Astronauts have talked of their profound awareness of the fragility of our tiny planet as they looked back at it from outer space. Here, I am still on earth but nonetheless powerfully possessed by that same feeling of physical separation and isolation from the sphere of human activity. For the moment, though, I am too preoccupied with survival to continue this train of thought.

I set off on a tour around Nake Islet. I cross a large sandy beach that borders the perfectly clear water of the lagoon until I am stopped in my tracks by a large circular clearing that runs from the beach into the forest, possibly created by high flooding tides during storms. It's so round, flat and clean that it doesn't look natural. It would make an ideal secure landing place for an extraterrestrial's flying saucer, a UFO. This fearful thought sends a shiver down my spine and I smile to myself, thinking that I've finally escaped society only to run into an alien race.

I hurry to the fresh openness of the east coast and walk along the tide's high water line. Here I'm reminded all too clearly that the world, with all its detritus, is always with us. I have to pick my way through the clutter of floating debris and litter that has been swept here from distant 'civilisations': bottles of gin, whisky, gallon demijohns and wine bottles by the score. Do we really consume so much alcohol? I step around polypropylene ships' hawsers and tangled bunches of fishing nets while large glass fishing balls fall in line with long bamboo poles to form Morse code symbols all along the beach. Perhaps if I took the time to put the Morse code symbols into letters and words, they would spell out my future and rescue me from all the anxieties in my head. This island seems to be the perfect geographical location to fulfil what has become my dream of living in isolation.

So far so good. But I worry about Anne. Will she soften her resistance and come to terms with her anxieties about the children? I have to ask myself, has this whole project perhaps become my personal obsession, an irresponsible act that shouldn't include two young children? My only defence is that my original proposal had been to live on a deserted island. Not only had she agreed, it was her idea to add children to the equation. I have to believe she will eventually be faithful to her agreement.

The deciding factor could be something else altogether, however: whether or not we will be able to enter Blind Passage.

Chattering white fairy terns with round black eyes flutter over my head to break my thoughts. I press on with my walking circuit of Nake Islet. I pass large black frigate birds, which look like vultures with their long hooked beaks and red wattles. They stare steadily at me, unafraid, from their perches on the low branches. These are the settled residents of Caroline, and in acknowledgement of their established presence, I nod a polite hello as I pass. I rest awhile on the sand and watch the cloud of migrating terns wheel around and around above the lagoon. They, like us, are nomads who have searched out this last unspoilt refuge on earth to raise their children.

According to the chart, a sacred Polynesian temple platform exists on the west coast of Nake Islet. This marae, I've been told, could date back to the time of Jesus Christ when Polynesians either inhabited this island or used it as a stopover on their long canoe voyages from Tahiti to Hawaii. Remembering the strange round landing site I came across earlier, I imagine for a moment that this platform could alternatively have been left by ancient extraterrestrials, infiltrating their golden-skinned, black-haired species into these Pacific islands. Either way, I'm pleased when I find amongst the undergrowth some solitary pieces of coral that have remained standing upright, in formation, all these years.

I enter a jungle of sharp pandanus leaves, coconut fronds, low thick bushes and a solid tangle of vines. I begin to search for wells and a cistern, which are also marked on the chart. The going is difficult. I continue by crawling under the bushes, first on my knees, then on my belly. In this slow process I become engaged in nose-to-nose Eskimo greetings with the local land crabs.

Suddenly a huge, prehistoric, spider-like coconut crab blocks my way. His legs are at least twenty-four inches long, his round body twice the size of my hand. I watch his long excited feelers nervously twitch and rotate. His big menacing claws rise up aggressively (or defensively, perhaps) and he begins to paw the air like a bull preparing to charge. I poke at him in Ali Baba fashion with my machete and force him to back off just far enough so that I can slide by to make my escape.

I emerge from under the bushes to find I'm looking at a large concrete cistern. It stands alone, grey and foreign in the midst of all this jungle greenery. I find 1938, the year of my birth, neatly marked on the front. As I examine its rusted outlet pipe, I consider for some time who is ageing better. Inside is a muddy, murky, fermenting mixture of leaves and water. I also see hundreds of mosquito larvae. I'm disappointed to find mosquitoes, since I was hoping that Caroline, being so isolated, would have none. I've also seen numerous small coconut rats.

Working my way out of the jungle, I'm confronted by yet another large coconut crab. This time I have the advantage of space and time. Tonight's dinner is secured.

The fresh openness of the beach is pleasing. Hot and tired, I rest a moment on the high bank of coral, where I can see *Fleur d'Ecosse* roll comfortably as she rises high with a passing swell, then settles low in the following trough. I pass a nostalgic moment reminiscing about my many years of voyaging and the pleasures shared with my trusty boat. There were times when it got so rough I had to help her stay together, and times when I was so down she had to see me through the storm. It's been like a real marriage. Now she is our family home and has brought us together to this island.

I built *Fleur d'Ecosse* myself. Beginning with a bare hull twenty-eight feet long made from waterproof polyester resin and fibreglass, I moulded a watertight cover over the open cockpit, since my priorities were to be safe, dry and comfortable. I spent a little over one year in the building. I tightened up every last stainless steel nut and bolt, knowing that one day my life may depend on their security. I carefully lined up my sparkling new diesel to within one-thousandth of an inch. I set up an unusual but easy-to-handle wishbone ketch rig. I designed and sewed my own sails. In all it was a passionate love affair. Despite inches of Scottish snow covering the deck, down below in front of the cast iron wood-burning stove, I could dream. It was easy to imagine being underway, sailing under starry skies en route to far distant lands. The heat of the stove became the warmth of soft tropical winds, the wood smoke, the smell of remote and exotic islands.

I took her name from a Scottish folk song written by Roy Williamson, whom I had met briefly when, as one half of the popular singing duo The Corries, he had performed in our local town hall. His song compares the passion of today's flowers of Scotland with the old adventurous spirit which once kept Scotland an independent nation.

O Flower of Scotland, when will we see your like again,
That fought and died for your wee bit o' hill and glen,

And stood against him, proud Edward's army,
And sent him homeward tae think again.

'Flower of Scotland' seemed an appropriate name for
a boat being prepared for a grand adventure. Scotland's old
alliance with France clinched the translation into the
French language. I didn't know then that I, a Scot, would
have such a close alliance with a Frenchwoman. Long after
I had named the boat *Fleur d'Ecosse*, the song 'Flower of
Scotland' grew to be accepted as Scotland's unofficial
national anthem and is now faithfully sung by Scottish
supporters at every national occasion such as international
rugby or football matches.

It took four years to sail *Fleur d'Ecosse* around our relatively small planet. En route I visited more than a hundred
foreign ports, encountered many different cultures, worked
my way up small shallow rivers, passed through the world's
biggest canals and crossed each of our immense oceans.
Then, quite by chance, I visited a small Pacific coral atoll.
It was there, on the island of Ahe, that the seeds of all my
future plans were sown.

What I encountered there were a courageous primitive
people who still hunted for their daily food. An island where
total sharing between the family and the community was
the norm, where the old people were deemed wise and
everyone participated in the care of the young children.
What I found was all that I felt we had lost in today's
modern and sophisticated way of life: a respect for the fulfilment of the simple needs of that animal we call human.
The native Polynesians on this small island still adhered to
the basic values of being close as families and ensuring that
everyone somehow had their place.

Once accepted, a visitor is incorporated into this
extended family and provided with a share of the daily

necessities. One is surrounded by an atmosphere in which people are serious about the immediate business of survival, yet open and fun-loving in their everyday approach to life in general.

The tropical Pacific Ocean weather, I discovered, is a friendly companion. The trade winds blow with constant regularity, only rarely modified by a short period of calm or extra-strong winds. Occasional seasonal cyclones are a threat, but around Tahiti and its islands they are more the exception than the rule. The temperature day and night remains in the eighties. It rains fairly regularly and drinking water can be collected easily.

When I left Scotland I had envisioned some kind of limited period of voyaging after which my money would run out and it would be time to return to a 'normal' work routine. It was only after three years of cruising that I slowly realised that – provided I kept the boat off the reefs, did all my own maintenance, stayed away from bars and restaurants and caught fish regularly – I could continue my pleasant lifestyle indefinitely.

From Ahe, and my new passion to live around the Pacific islands, grew the desire to live away from the close society of people – even such an agreeable society as that on Ahe – in the total isolation of an uninhabited island. I wanted to be more than a well-treated visitor; I wanted a place of my own. The kind of hunter-gatherer life I envisioned would be aided by a fruit and vegetable garden and would comp-lement the store-bought food provided by my pension.

The question now churning around in my brain is: will lonely Caroline Atoll fulfil all the requirements of this burning desire of mine?

3

A Triumphant Entrance

I return to the stark reality of my immediate situation as I arrive back at the beach and face the barrier of surf between the reef and open sea. The foaming swells in front of me roar with continuing violence and shake me to my senses. When I came in to the shore, the swells were at least going in my favour. Going out, they will be against me.

I put the coconut crab and machete aboard and fix the oars in place, struggling constantly to hold the dinghy against the incoming seas. I stay there for what seems an eternity, waiting for just that right moment to chance suicide. 'Go, go!' I shout to the gods, whom I hold totally responsible for my madness.

I jump and flounder aboard, grab the oars and begin to row furiously. The backwash helps me for a brief moment: I make progress, then the next breaker arrives. Wham! Water pours aboard and I stop dead. The crab and machete slosh about in the flood around my feet. I start again and keep rowing at the speed of a Keystone Cops movie, feeling that same terrible fear of impending disaster. All my efforts become focused as I press on. Then suddenly it's calm. I am through the chaos, and I can now return sedately to my waiting yacht.

Anne helps me on board. Relieved to have me back and

pleased about the crab, she serves me a cup of comforting tea. I'm still a little in shock. 'So,' she asks, 'how is it?'

'It's everything I imagined and more,' I tell her. 'There are thousands of birds. The east beach is covered with useful materials. The marae is there. And I found the concrete cistern; it's in good condition.' I say nothing about the spooky clearing.

'The swells are getting bigger,' she warns. But I can feel her relaxing, some of the tension easing after being left alone for such a long time with total responsibility for the boat.

We spend five days looking in toward a shore that is so near and yet so far away. We amuse ourselves to quiet boredom watching the endless action of big swells exploding on the passive reef. For a change in scenery we weigh anchor and head down the west coast to South Islet. There we anchor onto the reef in the same style as before – only now we have experience and the advantage of being hardened cliffhangers.

My sole preoccupation now is Blind Passage. I have to prove to myself that, given favourable conditions – that is, moderate trade winds and no current – this pass is practical to both enter and exit. With anxiety my faithful companion, going ashore on South Islet is no easier than on Nake Islet. I trudge my way across the reef's shallow waters. A four-feet-long reef shark races toward me. His black fin, like a deadly knife, cuts a fine line through the flat surface of the water, and his high tail flashes to and fro in the sunlight. His wake is straight and forms an arrowhead pointing directly to my feet. My guidebook was apparently wrong about the timidity of these creatures. Then another shark appears on my other side. I watch in shocked amazement as these two race each other like guided torpedoes towards their common target, my feet.

I leap fully out of the water and fall on my back in the dinghy. My feet wave high in the air as both sharks pass right under me. The size and bulk of the dinghy is sufficient to confuse their small minds. They back off quickly; nevertheless they remain close by to escort me through their territorial waters until I reach the safety of South Islet beach.

Later, I figure out that in shallow water six to nine inches deep, these sharks sense only a splashing movement which, on their isolated reef, represents a fish in difficulties and possible food. When you confront them under water, they see your full size and are indeed timid.

Walking around to the south side of South Islet, I come across a wrecked yacht. For a moment I think it's the missing ketch that we were supposed to look for. But in fact it's a small sloop by the name of *Petrel* that I had expected to find here. Before leaving Papeete, when I was searching everywhere for information about Caroline, I came upon *Petrel*'s owner, Gary Mundel. Over a beer he gave me the details of his story.

'I was single-handed and heading from Tahiti to Hawaii,' he began. 'By my navigational fixes I calculated I was well to the east of Caroline. I even stayed up late to be sure I passed the latitude of the island. Then I went to bed. The next thing I knew I was being lifted up and hammered onto the reef. It was four o'clock in the morning and pitch black. Somehow I managed to cross the reef to the safety of the shore.'

Gary spent fifty days alone on the island. When I asked him if he had found any buildings or knew the conditions at the pass, he told me he had done no exploring. In his desperation he had spent each day sitting on the highest point of the beach gazing out to sea, waiting for a ship to appear. He erected a large flag, prepared a fire to use as a smoke signal and used pieces of sail to print a large SOS on the coral bank.

He was afraid the fish were poisonous, so ate only the small reef sharks and the coconut crabs. With his largest sail suspended between the coconut trees, he was able to catch enough water for survival. He slept in his inflated life raft, its canopy providing shelter from the rain. At night the high steep rubber sides of the dinghy acted as castle walls, protecting him from the marauding coconut crabs with their dangerous claws. Luckily, his vigil ended when a French survey ship, *Coriolis*, came to the island to collect water samples. Another reluctant Robinson Crusoe was rescued.

Judging from his many possessions which still lie untouched aboard his yacht, I feel sure nobody has visited the island since his rescue two years earlier. *Petrel* remains a sad wreck up on the coral beach where sand and water splash endlessly in and out of the large hole in her side. Her aluminium mast still stands on deck. I take some time to salvage a coil of nylon anchor rope, plus some small fenders, then head north towards Blind Passage.

I sink into a preoccupied daze. I'm not a shipwrecked sailor or a castaway; I'm voluntarily choosing to settle here and create an ideal life state. *Petrel* rests heavily on my mind, a sharp reminder of how easily an adventure can turn to tragedy. For myself, I do what I do aware of the risks as I take my chances. But with Anne and the children I must remain within certain limits of safety and security.

When I reach Blind Passage the tide is low and the reef is dry. I can walk right up to the solid coral along the sides of the pass and look quietly down into its clear blue water. There is no current. At the pass entrance the sea conditions look more reasonable than when we arrived. For a more detailed inspection of the depths in the channel, I need the dinghy and facemask. I wander across the shallows of the lagoon to collect the dinghy, dreaming that everything will work itself out.

I almost step on two huge stingrays that move only at the last moment to leave behind a large cloud of fine sand. Then I see another shark rushing in and almost at my feet. With no liferaft alongside as refuge, in shock I throw myself fully out of the water to float momentarily suspended and horizontal over his dark passing body. My heavy belly flop frightens him away a short distance, then he heads cautiously and steadily back. I stay quite still. Slowly I back off toward the beach. My new admirer follows each footstep with passionate intensity. Safely on the dry sand I crouch down and watch him grind to a stop as he runs out of water. No more than three feet apart, we gaze at each other. As our eyes meet, we share for a moment our separate presence in this universe and our mutual confusion.

Back at the pass, having collected the dinghy and mask, I row without difficulty right up to the entrance. I hang over the edge of the dinghy wearing the facemask. I'm looking at twenty or more sharks, between four and seven feet long, which become excited by my presence. They swim fast and aggressively right up to the dinghy, then turn away, often striking the rubber inflatable with their tails. I freeze, fearful that one will attack and close his jaws on my air balloon and Blind Passage will become my personal cul-de-sac.

After this first spontaneous frenzy their excitement calms a little. I estimate, with a quick look, that the entrance to the pass is about twenty feet deep and around thirty-five feet wide. Fish abound. As I drift slowly down this calm canal away from the sea, I gaze at parrotfish and groupers as they swim amid a forest of bright orange live coral the shape of miniature trees. This underwater foliage runs in a long belt along the centre of the channel.

I pass an enormous Napoleon fish. He is at least six feet long and rests motionless as he watches my every move through large, cow-like eyes. Three hundred yards from the sea and still a hundred feet from the lagoon the pass ends. It's calm and quiet – a perfect place to moor *Fleur d'Ecosse*. A turtle sticks his head above the surface to join me in my revived state of hope. It gives me a knowing look as if to say, 'Yes, this is a fine secure place to rest up awhile.'

Back on the boat, Anne only half listens to my description of the pass. I stress the fact that when the water is low there is no current. 'That means, of course,' I analyse, as much for myself as for her, 'that the current flows out only when the tide is coming in. The rising seas flood in over the barrier, crest, then run down toward the pass and make their way back out to sea. That's pretty unusual.'

'We're also low on fresh water,' is all she replies. I don't see any obvious connection to the interesting anomaly of the current at the pass. I do know we're short of drinking water, and I'm sure her tension and anxiety reflect that fact. Normally, we carry enough water for twenty days' voyaging. Ten days have passed since we left Tahiti, and as we have to allow at least seven days for our return, we have just three days left to try to enter the pass.

This pressure to do something is temporarily foiled the next day when we attempt to raise the anchor. 'It's stuck solid,' Anne shouts in exasperation from the foredeck. We are close in alongside the reef. I rush to the bow and fix the warp tight to its cleat as we sink into the next trough. The following rising swell puts an enormous strain on the warp. The nylon creaks and moans, then with an underwater explosion the anchor breaks free, and we're drifting onto the reef. With steps that appear to take forever, I fly back to the cockpit, each moment anticipating that final sensation of being lifted up high toward heaven only to be dumped into the hell of foaming surf.

The diesel motor labours and slowly responds in reverse. Each second seems like an hour as the power of the motor builds up and increases the revolutions of the propeller. We begin to move – away from the breakers, away from the reef and back out to the safety of the open sea. As we arrive at the pass, the sun is behind us and the coral edges of the entrance are clearly visible. As we circle close, I imagine my line of approach between the breaking swells. The waves are big, but the sea is not as chaotic as when we first arrived.

'Hang on,' I shout to Anne. 'We're going in!' Alexandre leaves his lookout at the back door and waits on the cockpit floor. Anaïs is sleeping safely below.

We approach the entrance at maximum speed. I try to glance behind to check the following wave, but the breakers at the entrance demand my full attention as we rush toward them. I say a silent prayer to the boat, to the racing motor and to the forces of the cosmos.

Outside the entrance we're picked up by a wave and swept far to the left. I heave hard on the steering to correct the course and imagine our destiny if the cord should choose this moment to break. We surf fast down the last mounting wave with only the minimum of directional control. Surrounded by the roar of breaking surf we rush in through the entrance. I have time to observe the north edge of solid coral pass much too close for comfort. I let out a long extended 'Yaaaa-hooooo!' in exultation at having entered this Blind Passage. I want to jump up and down with joy and excitement, but confine myself to an affectionate kiss for my faithful boat. From the bow Anne manages a grin of relief. The absolute calm and tranquillity inside this tiny pass is shocking to us in our heightened state of tension. We quietly negotiate our way along its full length to end up in the small shallow basin.

'Look, a turtle!' Alexandre cries as we slowly turn the boat around to face the wind. 'It's the same turtle I saw before,' I reply. 'It must live here.' Then I give the turtle an intimate glance as if to say, 'You see, I took your advice.'

Gently Anne places the anchor on the delicate forest floor below. I then arrange chains around the solid and dead coral that rims this small basin and attach mooring lines to the chains. Finally I bring the anchor back on deck and away from the fragile coral.

Anne immediately prepares Alexandre and Anaïs for going ashore. She puts on their pyjamas to protect them from the harsh sun, plastic reef shoes and coconut hats. They talk nonstop in anticipation of at long last being able to go ashore on the island. Kiki and Dou-Dou appear on deck to wait, patient and attentive, as I inflate the dinghy.

I remain aboard alone. I let the absolute peace of the boat intoxicate my battered senses. I close my eyes and relish the sensation that comes from knowing that I've penetrated the sacred passage of the purest island in the whole South Pacific. Caroline's arms enfold me.

4

We Lay Claim to Our Destiny

Anne is hammering on the side of the boat for help to lift the children back aboard. 'Look,' Alexandre says, 'feathers!' Anaïs proudly shows me a bleached-out lobster shell. Anne has an unusual bottle with a face imprinted into its dark glass and marked 'Chile' on the bottom. Her special find is a net containing three small, smoke-coloured glass fishing buoys.

The next day, after a blissfully calm night and solid sleep on a motionless and silent *Fleur d'Ecosse*, we all go ashore to look for the cistern on South Islet. The two stingrays are still lying quietly in the same place in the shallows. Alexandre wants to make them move. 'Keep away,' I say, 'let them be. They have a poisonous barb on their tails; and if you annoy them, they can swing it around and stick it in your leg.'

We circle around the rays. Lifting Anaïs high up on my shoulders, I tell her, 'Now you have to look for sharks.'

She looks around for a moment and then announces with authority, 'I don't see some!'

'Well, keep looking,' I say. 'Because we're going to train these sharks. When one comes close, we all throw pieces of coral to chase it away. Then they'll learn we're not for eating.'

'Maybe we can eat *them*,' Alexandre suggests, covering his fear with bravado.

It's fun being ashore together. When we become thirsty, Anne climbs a short coconut tree and throws down some green coconuts. Proudly she uses her machete in the Polynesian fashion, neatly slicing off the tops and serving us the pure sparkling coconut water. Then, with a quick samurai swipe, she chops the coconut neatly in two. We scoop out the delicate soft jelly inside.

The cistern is exactly where it's marked on the chart. It's not in as good condition as the one on Nake Islet. A large coconut tree overhead has for years been dropping its produce directly into this tank, and a thick, black mud of decomposing coconuts and leaves half fills the inside. Parts of the walls are chipped and broken.

Water storage is very important for us. Our maths teacher quickly calculates that this tank could hold around 5000 litres of water. It's more than enough for our needs, but I'm afraid the walls are soft and could be porous. Near the base I find a large hole where the outlet pipe has rusted away.

I climb inside, slowly sinking up to my waist in the soft sticky sludge. Surrounded by mosquitoes and using only a piece of driftwood, I shovel out around two tons of dirty, smelly mud. Needless to say, I'm black from head to toe. 'Now you're beginning to look like a real Polynesian,' Anne says with one of her grins. Only when I've spread this huge pile of decomposed vegetation over a square area alongside the tank do I respond: 'Look! The Polynesian creates his first garden in the jungle.'

She doesn't answer, and I can hardly see her through the thick smoke of a large fire she has made to keep the mosquitoes away.

For our meal she has carefully cut out the centre core of a young coconut tree. This is the millionaire's heart-of-palm salad. She roasts a coconut crab in the embers of her fire, and we move out to the beach to settle down on a carpet of green coconut leaves for our first meal on Caroline.

Together we swim in the small channel that runs along the beach, then stretch out under the shade for a siesta. The wind is cool and soon the children are fast asleep. It's so truly peaceful here. No cars, no aircraft, no generators, no people. I close my eyes and hear only the constant low rumble of the surf; the shimmering hiss of the long narrow coconut leaves as the wind disturbs their rest; the ever-present cry of the birds, sometimes sharp and aggressive, sometimes passive; and the sudden splash of a frightened fish followed by the wild thrashing of an attacking shark. To this we later add our own sounds: the steady chip-chop of an axe, the crackle of fire, our voices calling through the jungle, and the hoarse and high-pitched laughter of the children. We hate to leave, but we need to return to the boat to sleep.

Ashore the next day we find an old ruined hut fairly close to the tank. All that remains is a collapsed and rotted tongue-and-groove floor plus some treated two-by-four floor beams. The beams may be usable. The corrugated roofing lies scattered around under the leaves. I collect a number of these sheets and clean them down before I realise they are made from aluminium and, apart from a few corrosive pinholes, are in good condition.

The children find various pots and pans, plus a bottle still containing uncooked rice. I come across two large rolls of zinc about eighteen inches wide, which I guess to be about forty feet long. This material is usually placed in a band around the trunks of the coconut trees to stop the rats from climbing up to eat the fresh coconut buds. Around the hut I find only four trees that have been banded. Alongside an old broken box we find some pieces of rusted chain and a wooden boat's pulley. Close to the beach we come across an axle with two heavy cast-iron wheels and a solid rubber tread. I push one wheel, and it still turns. I wonder why and for what purpose this axle was brought here. I've seen no roads on the island, not even a track.

With our fresh water supply running out, we have to think about leaving Caroline, though we've only been here for two days. And what about returning? Anne, after much discussion, is still not totally committed to the idea of settling here. She does, however, acknowledge that it's a beautiful island. 'Okay, I'll give it a try,' she says at last. I sigh quietly with relief.

We begin to empty the boat of all its supplies so as to gain maximum space aboard for provisions and tools we'll acquire in Tahiti. Carefully we place everything in the newly cleaned-out tank until the inside begins to look like the shelves of a supermarket. Cans of butter, milk, fish, vegetables and fruit are arranged and stacked up in neat rows. The final item is our Singer hand-sewing machine, which has always been on the boat. I used it first to sew all our sails, then to make our cushion and mattress covers. Now we use it to make our clothes. It's precious and I'm reluctant to leave it, but it takes up important storage space and is heavy. Finally, I cover the tank with the salvaged corrugated aluminium sheets and place large pieces of coral on top.

Before laying the last sheet on, we write out a short note and place it inside:

We leave these supplies, as very soon we intend to settle on Caroline Atoll. Everything is important for our survival here. If you really need something, help yourself: otherwise, please leave us our precious stores.

Ron, Anne, Alexandre and Anaïs Falconer

Finally, Alexander and Anaïs clean out the cooking pots they've found and place them alongside the tank. Together we slope the few remaining corrugated sheets along the side of the tank into these containers. Hopefully rainwater will collect and we will have some fresh water on our return. In the mud garden I plant some papaya seeds – the large, sweet, yellow fruit that grows so abundantly in the tropics – as a symbolic gesture of establishing roots on the island. I tell the children, 'One day we're going to have a really big garden with lots of papayas, bananas, watermelon, tomatoes, cucumbers and everything that will grow here.'

Now that we have our plans set for returning, I can leave in peace and anticipation. Before going to sleep, Alexandre says thoughtfully, 'Wow, that was a good day.' Anaïs quickly adds, 'I had a good day too.' I repeat her sentence and finally so does Anne. This way of checking in with each other each night will become our ritual on Caroline. Our definitions of what a good day consists of may differ, but almost always we have a consensus of satisfaction.

Everything is in its place for going to sea. The motor is warm and the children and animals are below. 'Okay, let's go!' I shout, focusing my inner forces to exit the pass safely. We drop the mooring lines and slowly build up to maximum speed. The exit approaches. I see the tall steel pole with a gear wheel on top that I found on South Islet and that now marks the entrance. I wonder how long it will stand up against the continual battering of the waves.

'Hold on!' I cry to the children below as we rise up and over the first ocean swell. The boat rolls wildly. We lose a little speed. The second wave is less steep, and we exit safely into the moderate east trade wind. We shut the motor down, set the sails, and run before the wind with the automatic pilot in control. Our carefree days on the island were too short, and we are all a little saddened to be back on the open sea with several days' sailing ahead.

Although we're low on drinking water, we can't yet

abandon our search for that missing yachtsman. Besides
looking for him on Caroline, we have also agreed to search
two other small, uninhabited islands in this area called
Vostok and Flint. Vostok lies one hundred miles to the west
of Caroline, and Flint a further one hundred miles to the
south.

The yachtsman was in fact the final coincidence in a
series which enabled us to start this expedition. Originally
we had left France with the intention of sailing directly to
an island called Suvarov in the Pacific Ocean, an atoll
where a hermit, Tom Neale, had lived for several years.
I'd met Tom and also visited Suvarov. As we made our way
toward Suvarov, however, somewhere around the Panama
Canal, Anne became pregnant. This put a temporary stop to
our fine planning. We headed for Ahe, where I had been
made so welcome on my first visit. There we would be
within overnight sailing distance of a small hospital on
nearby Rangiroa.

On Ahe, Alexandre was born, and Anaïs came two years
later. Since life on this lovely island was pleasant and
comfortable, we could have been lulled into staying there
forever, or at least for a long time. Because of visa problems
with the Cook Island Government the plan to settle on
Suvarov wasn't possible. But I hadn't quite given up my
dream, and in one of my periodic searches for the ideal
deserted island I came across a dot on the South Pacific
Ocean nautical chart which simply said 'Caroline'. This
lonely coral atoll, crescented like a new moon, lay ten
degrees south of the equator in the centre of a huge stretch
of nearly a million square miles of isolated ocean.

The South Pacific Pilot Book said that it was around
seven miles long by one mile across. It had a small lagoon
and a possible safe place for the boat, which could be
reached by Blind Passage. Most important, it hadn't been

inhabited for over one hundred years. The Pilot Book stated that the atoll was originally a British possession but now belonged to the recently formed Republic of Kiribati, and is at present under a private lease to a Captain Omer Darr, who lives on the island of Moorea, next to Tahiti.

It sounded perfect, but again it might have remained only a dream had I not encountered Dave, a yachtsman visiting Ahe, who told me that he knew Captain Darr personally and would be meeting him when he reached Tahiti.

'Ask the captain if he'd be interested in acquiring a guardian for his island,' I suggested casually as we parted.

Shortly after this meeting we ourselves happened to be in Tahiti. I met Dave by chance outside the post office in downtown Papeete. We chatted for some time as yachties do and had said our goodbyes when he suddenly turned around and added, 'Oh, by the way, I spoke to Captain Omer Darr and he's interested in your proposal. Go and see him – he lives at the Shark's Tooth Boutique on Moorea.'

The next day I caught the ageing ferry boat that chunters daily across the ten-mile stretch of ocean between Tahiti and Moorea.

Captain Darr was in his sixties and carried the upright bearing of an English gent. He told me that once he had sailed all over the Pacific Ocean as captain of the old inter-island sailing schooners. Now shorebound, he lived quietly in his small, smart bungalow by the sea. He had indeed obtained a 25-year lease on Caroline Atoll from the British government back in 1964 which the present Kiribati government agree to honour. And he *was* interested in a guardian. He wrote a letter then and there giving us, for a start, his permission to visit the island. I was elated, even though his final words were: 'Remember, Ron, if by chance you put your boat on the reef, no one is there to help you!'

My elation was somehat calmed later by Anne's attitude
against isolating the children still further from medical care.
Ahe already lies two hundred miles to the north of Tahiti,
and Caroline is another three hundred miles further toward
the equator. She insisted that we should do our shopping as
we had planned and head back to Ahe. I might have agreed,
but as I was waiting to fill up our water containers at the
only tap in the anchorage, I met Paul, a young American
who lived aboard a fine old wooden yacht. Naturally, I
started talking about Caroline.

'Did you say Caroline Atoll, between here and Christmas
Island?' he asked.

'That's the one,' I answered. 'It lies exactly ten degrees
south of the equator.'

'That's really strange,' he said. 'We had a friend who left
here six months ago to sail alone to Hawaii, but he never
arrived. His name is Manning and his yacht is *Marara*. Right
now we and his family are trying to organise a boat party
to search Caroline Atoll. A medium told us he was close to
turtles and on a coral island.' Paul said that he would pay us,
provided we would also check out Flint and Vostok, the two
other uninhabited atolls in that same area.

For me, this was enough. An ideal island existed, it was
available, we had transport and permission to visit, plus we
would be paid. Excitedly, I conveyed this information to
Anne. She replied simply, 'I thought we were going back
to Ahe – that was the plan.'

'Well, it was, but don't you think destiny is playing her
own hand?'

'Not my idea of destiny,' she responded with an annoyed
sigh. 'Oh well, I'm not sure about this, but I know you: once
you've made up your mind I guess I'm stuck with it.' Anne
enjoys adventuring and I suspected she was hiding a conflict
between her own excitement and her fears for the children.

Little did we know at that moment what fortuitous fate had handed us. Or that fate was going to put significant obstacles in our way.

Vostok, no more than a raised lump of coral a few hundred yards in diameter, is represented on the ocean chart as the merest dot. It's an overnight sail from Caroline, and we arrive off the island just before midday. As on Caroline, we anticipate a mythical Robinson Crusoe-like figure running out from the bushes waving a ragged shirt, but no one comes. There is no barrier reef, so with the dinghy, I surf directly onto the coral beach, accompanied by the now familiar escort of a black-tipped shark.

There are no coconut trees on Vostok. Other tall green trees stand together to form a small forest on this otherwise barren block of coral. Inside the forest it's quite dark. A black humus of decomposed leaves forms a spongy flat floor between the trees. My first thought is that I could always come here to collect soil for Caroline's garden.

I stand still among the trees for a long time, letting my deeper senses communicate with the silent power of this rare, isolated place. For thousands of years this island has existed beyond the dreams of man. Here, the plants blossom and die only for themselves, the birds perform their love dances for each other alone and the insects commit their dastardly deeds without judgement. This is the world I love, the world that you can always sense when sailing a small boat on a vast ocean. And it feeds the spiritual hunger that has been nagging my body and soul for fulfilment. Touching this pure and exotic world, I feel a desperate need to join the fine dance of life that surrounds me. Not as the grand director, but as one of the chorus of lowly dancers, moving to the rhythm and music of the sun, the moon, the stars, the winds and the rains. This is what it is to be alive and to sense directly the profound forces of existence which are made banal by the modern way of life.

Back on the beach I find large, sun-bleached wooden planks which lie in a line along the high water mark. A solid cast-iron motor rests amid the shallow coral as a reminder of the other world. I wonder if the bones of any long-marooned sailors (including the yachtsman Manning, perhaps) lie here to rest forever in this tranquil grave.

It takes less than an hour to complete my tour around the island. In the meantime Anne has been sailing the boat to and fro off the island. It's the first time she has sailed *Fleur d'Ecosse* unaided. I watch approvingly as she manoeuvres close alongside the dinghy and stops with complete precision, a broad smile on her face.

We sail on to Flint Island, which, like Caroline, was inhabited for a short time one hundred years ago. At that time the settlement was established to export guano, a rich fertiliser comprised of bird droppings. The island is around three miles long and one mile across, but has no lagoon. As we arrive, we pass a large square tower on the beach that marks the old landing place.

As I look in toward the bare beach, I remember that Captain Darr told me he had seen a pack of wild dogs here. I add to Alexandre's excitement by saying, 'Look for wild dogs as well as the wreck.'

'Real wild dogs?' he asks.

'Well, not really. They're normal dogs that were left here on the island and then went wild.'

'Then they're just dogs,' he says with a shrug.

'Yes, they're just dogs,' I agree, 'but normal dogs are trained and controlled. If they were here alone for a long time, they'd go back to their wild ways. They could attack us like sharks.'

'Whooow,' he says, 'that's real wild dogs.'

The wind has been slowly strengthening since our

arrival, and the waves are growing uncomfortably high. We've completely circled the island and seen no wreck, no humans, and no dogs. To compensate, I let Alexandre blow the foghorn over and over again just in case someone remains hidden among the trees.

It's too rough to go ashore. We rest awhile off the north-east point of the island, eat a light meal and watch the steadily deteriorating conditions.

'Look,' Alexandre says, 'there are two turtles playing. One's climbing on the back of the other.'

'Maybe it's a mummy with a baby on her back,' Anaïs says.

I smile innocently. In my opinion, the turtles are mating, though I'm not really sure how turtles copulate. For the moment I have more pressing problems. The wind has increased to over thirty knots and is dead ahead for our course back to Tahiti. There is no sheltered anchorage here, so we have no alternative but to sail out into the wind and battle against the high waves and surface currents. With no supplies and little water or fuel aboard, the boat is too light.

The conditions are bad. With only the working jib and mizzen staysail set, we begin to fly off the tops of the steep waves and crash heavily into the deep troughs. It's terrible. Slowly, as the hours of violence continue, we are gradually reduced to a zombie-like state where even the slightest activity aboard becomes a major undertaking.

To various degrees we are all seasick. Anne is the least affected and Anaïs is the worst. Alexandre and I have vomited, but remain fairly stable. We don't eat and try to drink regularly so as not to get dehydrated. Anaïs, who is vomiting almost continually, is the one who risks suffering dehydration most acutely. Anne spends her time comforting Anaïs and insists that she keep taking small sips of water mixed with some sugar and a little salt. We try to amuse ourselves, but the conditions are too rough for reading or any thought of playing games. We lie quietly in our respective beds, each absorbed in his or her physical discomfort. We try to reassure each other but our words run dry. There is little we can do, so we try to remain calm in the face of adversity. The immediate health of the children, along with the safety of the boat, is our most important priority. I also worry about Anne. Will this unfortunate and untimely voyage turn her against our whole project to return to Caroline?

Day after day we tack a hundred miles across the wind in gale force conditions to get only thirty miles closer to our destination. In our misery we switch on our small transceiver radio and tune in to what has become our regular local radio network.

'Monday morning coffee klatch. Any more check-ins for the Monday morning coffee klatch?' I recognise the voice of Little Earl, an American who operates from his boat in Tahiti. I press my transmit button and give my call sign.

'Ron, good morning. How are things with you?' He's relaxed and cheerful, and I envy him his calm anchorage.

'It's rough, Earl. It's blowing a gale out here. We're all right, but it's not at all comfortable.'

'I know. We have the same wind here. It's what the locals call the Maaramu. It's a little south of southeast, strong and steady, bringing up cold air from Antarctica. Anything we can do for you this morning?'

'Yes – if it's possible, I'd like to contact Paul and Sophia on the *Denebola*.'

'No problem,' he's quick to reply. 'They're close by me here in Maeva Beach. I'll call them on the VHF.'

'Okay, Earl. Can you tell them that we've checked out the three islands, Caroline, Vostok and Flint, for the missing yacht *Marara* and found no sign of it?'

'Roger, roger. Stand by a few minutes. Pick up Les, and I'll get back to you.'

Les is another American yachtsman who now lives ashore on Moorea. His familiar deep, gravelly voice enters the boat and has a comforting effect on our distress.

'Morning, Ron, sorry to hear you're having such a rough trip. How are Anne and the children?'

'We're surviving, Les, but I wish this wind would drop a little or change direction, anything to ease this night and day battle.' Les is sympathetic and we continue discussing our suffering, until Earl breaks back into the conversation.

'I've talked to Paul, Ron. He sends his regards. He told me that *Marara* has just been found. It seems a Korean fishing boat came across the yacht drifting one thousand miles to the southwest of Hawaii. The sails were torn, but otherwise the boat was undamaged. When the fishermen went aboard, they found his skeleton remains still sitting at his dining table. They towed the yacht back to Hawaii. The experts have reached no conclusion as to the cause of death.'

'Well, that's news,' I reply in surprise and shock. We knew Manning only by photo, but he had become part of our expedition, and we really hoped we might have found him alive. Now that he's dead, our already depressed spirits dive even lower. I thank Earl for his help and switch off the radio.

What could have happened to Manning? He was a fairly young man with considerable experience on a well-fitted boat. Visions of a *Marie Celeste* situation cross my mind. Back in the days of the old square-rigged sailing ships, the *Marie Celeste* was discovered becalmed out on the open sea. All her sails were set, but when the ship was boarded, nobody was found. Down below, the breakfast table was still set, and the boarders claimed the food was still warm. This left the big question: what had happened to the crew? Well, at least Manning's body was found.

The wind blows hard and steady for a total of eight days; then it just stops. The sky clears, and we have our first accurate navigation fix since leaving Flint Island. We discover we are fifty miles to the west of Bora-Bora, and still two hundred miles from Tahiti. We use the last of our fuel to motor over the now smooth swells and arrive ten hours later inside Bora-Bora's calm lagoon.

In the morning, still weak but somewhat revived from a calm night's sleep, we fill up with fresh water, fresh fruit, fresh vegetables, general supplies and fuel. Anne is especially exhausted, and in consideration of her feelings, I decide to take a leisurely island-hop back to Tahiti.

5

Preparations for a Long Stay

Our first stop on the way to Tahiti is Raiatea. Just as we begin to enter its small marina, I recognise a red yacht moored outside the entrance. 'Look!' I call out to Anne. 'It's *Tamata*!' As we come alongside, I shout, 'Anyone aboard?' It's quiet, but Bernard's distinctive, tractor inner-tube dinghy is tied up to the stern.

Just as I fear he may be asleep, his head pops up through the hatch, and my memory flashes back to the day ten years ago when I first met Bernard. It was during my first stay on Ahe. As I was standing with Arii, the young village chief, we watched a large black ketch sail slowly past the end of the village quay. Quietly we admired the lone captain strutting on deck, adjusting sails and steering with a sense of familiarity among the many coral heads. He finally anchored in a sheltered corner. As he passed, I could read *Joshua* painted in large letters on the stern. 'Who's that?' I asked Arii.

'That's Bernard Moitessier; he's French and a writer,' Arii explained.

The name was familiar. Somewhere in the long distant past, when I was devouring every last sailing and adventure story I could find, trying desperately to identify with the character of the writer and find for myself that mysterious power called courage, I had read one of Moitessier's books, *The Long Way*. It was an account of the very first single-handed, nonstop race around the world. What I remember most about the story is that at one point he had a chance to win the race but dropped out and headed back to the peace of the Pacific islands.

As time passed on Ahe, I slowly came to know Bernard. At first we would nod a polite hello when we both participated in the regular football matches. Then we exchanged a few words at the periodic village feasts and at the monthly supply boat while waiting to do our shopping. It was only when we agreed to get together to practise in private the local sport of throwing spears at a coconut attached to a pole high off the ground that we really got to know each other. Our harmless practising turned into a clash between gladiators who competed with terrible concentration to outdo one another. We went spearfishing together and built a fish trap. Eventually, we met fairly regularly at his hut, where we shared meals and spent time working in his garden.

Perhaps because we were both independent loners, we never became truly intimate friends. Bernard's passion, energy and commitment to his island life was nevertheless an important inspiration, an example to me of a non-Polynesian who had gone native. Bernard also played a key role in our destiny by leading me to the hermit Tom Neale and thus ultimately to Suvarov. Bewitched by the spell of lonely Suvarov, I promised myself that one day I too would live on an uninhabited island.

After Ahe, Bernard sailed to America. There, during a sudden storm, the *Joshua* was swept onto a beach in Mexico. He's now back in the Pacific with his new, smaller yacht *Tamata*. Pleased to see us, he smiles warmly as we pass our lines and organise fenders between the two boats. We have never been aboard *Tamata*, and I'm surprised to find how tidy, open and spacious it is below decks.

'First a cup of tea, or maybe a tisane,' Bernard shyly suggests, unpacking a tiny Primus pressure stove that's stowed away in a cupboard and which, with some sense of ceremony, he places on its bench and then ties down with small chains. Next he fills a small kettle and adjusts more chains to hold the kettle in place. I watch and wonder why he doesn't have a simple swinging stove common to almost every small boat that sails offshore on the open sea. Then I remind myself once more that Bernard is Bernard, and Bernard has his own special way of doing everything. The tea is good and he brings out biscuits for the children, but the falling crumbs disturb him. He sits patiently with a small plastic brush and shovel, collecting each crumb as it tumbles down to offend his clean painted floor.

We reminisce about our life on Ahe and all our common friends there. He tells us he's making progress on his latest book, *Tamata and the Alliance*. At this moment he's waiting for his girlfriend, Veronique, to return from Paris.

Then we talk about Caroline. Immediately interested, he pulls out his ocean chart. 'There!' I put my finger on the chart. 'Between the Marquesas, Penrhyn, and Christmas Island. Rangiroa is the nearest inhabited island.'

'Any buildings or roads?' he asks.

'No buildings, no roads. There are two concrete tanks – that's all.'

He wants to know about the fishing, birds, mosquitoes, rats, coconut crabs, lobsters and turtles. 'And fruit?' he continues. 'Are there any fruit trees?'

'No fruit trees.'

'And a well. Did you find a well?'

'I found two holes, but they were filled in with rubble.'

I explain about the pass. At once he appreciates the

unusual phenomenon of the outgoing current confronting the incoming tide. We work out a timetable for low water according to the stages of the moon. 'New moon or full moon would be the best times to arrive,' I explain. 'Low water would then be around mid-morning and the sun would be behind you as you enter the pass.'

Like me he is attuned to that kind of thinking – programming events to the position of the moon and the sun. I draw out a sketch of the pass, with distances and depths, and locate my marker on the north side of the entrance. Bernard is now really excited and enthusiastic. We explain our immediate program, and I know we can expect him soon for a visit to Caroline.

It's another day's sail to Huahine, from where we are obliged to sail overnight to Moorea. There we anchor close to the Shark's Tooth Boutique, where Captain Omer Darr can be found. Captain Darr holds a special attraction for the children: he owns an ice-cream booth. Into the free ice-cream we mix free bananas that hang up along his booth for visitors.

'You were brave to enter Blind Passage,' he says as our story unfolds one more time.

'Brave or foolish, I can't decide,' I reply honestly.

'As you know, my present lease runs out in two years' time,' he explains. 'I'm trying hard to renew it at this moment, but Caroline is now part of the new Republic of Kiribati, and their government doesn't reply to my letters.'

Hearing this report, I feel a first shiver of apprehension. For us, two years is not long enough to justify moving islands and building a new settlement. He says he will keep trying to renew his lease and is confident that, once he communicates with the new government, he will be successful. He carefully types out a formal agreement that under his lease I am legally appointed the guardian of Caroline Atoll. There will be no payment, and we are to be responsible for our own health, welfare, and belongings; 'in full knowledge of the dangers of residing on an isolated island', he adds. He calls in his house help and the girl from the boutique to sign the agreement as official witnesses. For the time being, he agrees to hold our mail. If necessary, we will communicate by radio through our common friend Les on Moorea.

Over a glass of wine we talk for quite some time about our experiences with the sea and the Pacific islands. 'I wouldn't give permission to just anyone,' he comments eventually. 'It's because of your previous experiences and awareness that I think you'll be all right. Caroline is one of the last unspoiled places left on the planet, and I know you'll keep it that way.

'It was my dream to retire there,' he confides quietly, and with a little sadness. 'For me it didn't work out. My wife Harriet finds even Moorea too isolated. I wish you well.' I am moved by this confidence and the brief moment of sharing our spirits in the fateful pull of Caroline. As the children finish one more ice-cream, we formally shake hands. Anne and I say our goodbyes, content with our paper agreement.

In Papeete we share a meal aboard the *Denebola* with Paul and Sophia. Manning's death remains another mystery of the sea. It's a little frightening, and we can do nothing except share their sadness at the loss of a good friend. Before we leave they pay us our fee for the search. For once we have extra money, enough for a six-month supply of food and all the materials we need to buy. Plus a little something left over for a cold beer.

Despite our terrible journey from Flint Island, Anne remains faithful to her commitment to try to settle on Caroline. She goes ashore to start the shopping. I remain aboard with the children preparing the boat for the coming supplies. By mid-morning the boxes of food begin to arrive: powdered milk, tinned butter, cans of vegetables and fruit, honey, coffee, tea, dried beans and lentils, packets of sugar and a sack of flour. All the lockers are quickly filled and the boxes pile up on the floor. Anne returns with medical supplies: aspirin, plasters, bandages, antibiotics, anti-diarrhoea and anti-dehydration powders, and contraceptive cream. She finishes her list with items like toothpaste, shampoo, soap, lice shampoo, worm tablets, clothes pegs, candles and matches.

Now it's my turn to shop. I buy a pick and shovel, a large crowbar, a bushman's saw, a large axe, a small axe, three solid machetes, a hammer and a large tarpaulin. I include one luxury item: twelve floorboards, twelve feet long by twelve inches wide, for our jungle house. I find a sack of cement, plus a new brass tap and galvanised pipe to repair the cistern. I finish with a few kilos of assorted galvanised nails.

I also buy some hens and a cock from a family just outside Papeete. They find it very amusing that someone on a yacht should be buying hens. We agree on a price, and with wide smiles they help me choose five young hens and a healthy cock. We put the hens in a box and tie it to the back of the bicycle I have borrowed. As I look back for a final goodbye, they stand waving, their grins fully spanning the distance between their ears. My final purchase is a full roll of chicken wire for a chicken run and a roll of more sturdy mesh for cages.

'Come on,' I say to Alexandre and Anaïs. 'We have to make a wire mesh box to fit in the toilet compartment for the hens.' They help by holding the sides upright while I attach the top and bottom. Soon we fit the large cage into its place and lay out newspapers on the bottom.

Having hens aboard is an amusing distraction for the

children. The new arrivals are fed and watered continually until the excitement dies down and our hens become part of the crew and team for this expedition. The parakeets aloofly ignore their feathered neighbours. Not so Dou-Dou, who appoints herself official guardian. After a long examination of her captives, she passes her day in surveillance, stretched out close to their cage. As the days pass the smell below decks becomes more and more noticeable and our desire to leave more urgent.

As usual, the customs and immigration officials are friendly; they are amused by each development in our story. They smile as they photocopy our agreement with Omer Darr. With handshakes and warm wishes of good luck, once more we receive our clearance papers for Caroline Atoll.

We visit Ahe on our way north. When we arrive, our Polynesian friends wonder where we've been for so long. When we tell them the full story, one family offers to pack up their things then and there and come along with us. I'm glad I can say that the boat is full, because for the time being I prefer to be alone.

On Ahe we left our twelve-foot long aluminium dinghy, which we call *Mini-Mini*. I want to take it along with us, but it's too big to carry on deck. The only solution is to tow it all the way to Caroline behind the boat. First, we load it with our plastic barrels and light water containers, then cover the whole load by tying on our new tarpaulin.

Mama Fana, the wife of the old chief, who in the past has let us use her nine-horsepower outboard motor for *Mini-Mini*, now insists we take it with us to Caroline. Certainly a fast, practical runabout would be useful on the lagoon. But I politely refuse, as I have already decided that living on Caroline will be an ideal chance to exist without the disturbance of the internal combustion engine. The motor on *Fleur d'Ecosse* is necessary, but I don't want one on our island home. Although for health and safety reasons we plan to incorporate some non-primitive adaptations, I draw the line at objects that do not contribute to the peaceful life we seek.

Mini-Mini with sails, leeboard and a steering oar is sufficient transport for our silent lagoon. We have no schedules to keep, and the regular trade wind will move us where and when we please. For electricity we have our solar panels, which are also quiet and efficient. Mama Fana quickly understands. She points to a large, abandoned, clinker-built boat alongside her house. 'In the old days Papa Toa and I used to travel to all the other atolls with only sails. Now the young people know only the motor.'

We transfer our belongings from our hut onto *Fleur d'Ecosse*: mattresses, blankets, pillows, mosquito netting, a kettle, pans, dishes, a wash basin, plastic buckets, large storage tins and the metal bars that support the pots over an open fire. To supplement the garden seeds we bought in Papeete, we take seeds given to us by the village people. Included are species of tomato, green beans, Chinese cabbage, cucumber and watermelon, all of which have proven themselves not only nutritious but capable of surviving in the poor coral atoll soil. Soon it is time to continue on our way. The hens, who have spent their time in a temporary run during our preparations, now return to their cage below decks.

Before we're allowed to leave we're given a typical Polynesian farewell as necklaces of sweet-smelling flowers are hung around our necks. The Polynesians, always great orators, enter fully into our adventures with long speeches that express their respect and attachment to their islands, families and friends. We are made to feel special and a real part of the Ahe community. The ceremony finishes with warm hugs and kisses from every last person in the village.

We are sad to leave this precious island. This is where we learned all of our island ways and shared so much with these open and friendly Polynesian people, feeling part of one big family. We have been included in all the village activities, from the birth of a baby to the funeral of one of the old wise men. Almost every day we played basketball or football together. Each evening we made music and talked on the quay until our eyes refused to stay open and we would fall asleep once more to the sweet soft sounds of guitars and rich singing of voices in perfect harmony. Absorbed in our rich memories, we cross the lagoon for the last time, *Mini-Mini* doesn't share our quiet reflections; in rebellious reaction she tugs on her towrope and drags reluctantly behind, as if unhappy to leave the familiar surroundings of her lagoon.

We settle down for what should be a pleasant, three-day sail. But *Mini-Mini* continues to be difficult. First she careens way off to one side, then to the other, before her towrope snaps her bow back into line. Often she is picked up by a wave and surfs past us, dragging her rope alongside. In desperation I add a heavy chain to her nylon towrope. She remains difficult but is somewhat subdued.

It's two months since we left Caroline. Two months of organisation were required to prepare for this long period of isolation. Now that we are en route with a moderate wind and comfortable seas there is little to do aboard. Our recent bad voyage, if not forgotten, has been laid aside. In good spirits, we slowly head north to our destination and spend our time amusing the children.

'One, two, three,' I start our familiar game.

'One, two, three,' they repeat after a little hesitation.

'Un, deux, trois,' the French teacher adds.

'Un, deux, trois,' the children reply, having no trouble whatsoever in clearly separating the two languages. They are totally bilingual and often a conversation around the table embraces both languages. They address and answer me in English, while for their mother they revert to French. When I met Anne my understanding of the French language, apart from *bonjour*, was zero. Since Anne had taken English in school, she communicated with me in that language. Before long she became totally comfortable in English, while my knowledge of French remained nonexistent. Years later when I did speak reasonable French, the children continued to address me in English and could not get it into their heads that 'Pap' now understood French.

We keep watch through the night, but there are no squalls, no ships and no islands on our course. All is quiet aboard and the tropical nights slide by agreeably, the stars shine brilliantly overhead and the moon follows the path of the sun from east to west. I take the early morning watches as I really enjoy this special time when the darkness pales into blue, and the sky begins to lighten rose with the promise of another warm, perfect day. This is the time when I gather courage and imagine that all our efforts will be worthwhile and that all our desires will be fulfilled. It's a time to reflect, question motivations, and face up to the reality of what I'm doing.

I'm on my way, yearning for time and peace away from organised human society. I need this distance to begin approaching the basic motivating force that I know for certain lies deep inside me, a force strong enough to drive a reasonable person to live in isolation on a desert island. It's going to be a slow process uncovering that source of pure energy.

The dynamic force of physics that pulls floating atoms together and has created our universe fascinates me. It surrounds and exerts its all-powerful pull on everything around us. It draws things together to create and recreate, over and over again, in a never-ending cycle that knows no end, only the path onward. Even when its creations die, explode or burn out, as they inevitably do, this force will continue to pull what particles remain and rearrange them into some new basic creative block. The power and permanence of this dynamic force are reassuringly predictable, although some of its unkindly and unjust characteristics are not altogether agreeable.

This is the force that produced our planet and brought together the life spark which led on to the dinosaurs and finally arrived at us. Its only apparent motive is attraction and creation, whether it be a universe, a planet or the long evolution of living things. Everything, from simple cells to complex creatures, leads back to this common source. Each new creation is not only a representation of the force, but also contains the force within it. This is the drive that makes us fight to survive and move our individual lives forward.

However, the jungle of life is difficult. When we arrive as individuals we have no guaranteed place. We have to fight to make space for ourselves and hold on to it, to survive if we can for the duration of our life span. It's an intriguing system in which not only the strongest dominates, but where the smallest virus also competes in its own way. Periods of calm do exist when established forces momentarily settle into a restless peace. But the potential for change is constant. The competition and struggle can never stop.

As observant human beings, most of us recognise these facts, but being also of a sensitive nature, we don't particularly want to participate in what seems to be a futile and nonstop war of survival. Therefore, we go to great lengths to find ways – either practical, in the creation of laws that regulate society, or abstract, in the form of religion – to control the common enemy: our own natures. But our nature, for better or for worse, is fundamental to our survival, and modifying it too greatly could lead to our extinction.

In organised society the set changes, the actors change, but ultimately the war goes on. Now it's the dominating capitalists, power-seeking dictators or terrorists who have harnessed their energy best and use it to control an otherwise apathetic society. History teaches us that all our sincere, idealistic plans and dreams to create a gentler, kinder, peaceful working world order are doomed to failure by the actions of our own natures. This is the force that I want to examine, far from the cacophony and confusion of everyday society.

Somewhere there was a beginning; perhaps one day there will be an end. For the moment, that's not important. What is important, if we are to arrive at any sensible plan for the medium term, is that we honestly accept and confront this determined and bloody force. For me this is a day-to-day ongoing process that won't be rushed and is not simply intellectual. It's something sensitive and profound. I hope that with time I'll be able to validate my feelings about the properties of the force and touch its values directly through associating with nature. On another level, there could be a need to justify my personal actions toward Anne, which I fear may sometimes be overbearing.

These are the preoccupations that fill my mind and drive our little boat towards this island. As I watch the first rays of the rising sun push over the horizon, I take a long deep breath in anticipation of another fresh and untouched day.

I look forward to our isolation on Caroline. As it happens, though, we're in for a bit of a surprise when we get there.

6

Visitors Already

On the third day of sailing we sight the island at four o'clock in the afternoon. 'There's a yacht in the pass!' Anne cries as the island draws nearer.

It can only be Bernard and Veronique. My heart sinks. Much as I like them, I'd hoped we would have time to settle in before they came. I now recognise the red hull of *Tamata* as she sits upright and quiet inside the reef. Outside the entrance we have another problem. The late afternoon sun is shining directly into our eyes, so that even with our dark Polaroid sunglasses the reflection from the sea is blinding and I can see neither my marker nor the coral edges of the entrance. As I slowly circle in front of the pass, I see Bernard and Veronique, tiny stick figures against the white sand, emerging from the forest and walking across the beach.

'It's too dangerous to enter with this light,' I tell Anne as we circle one more time around the entrance. 'We'll have to wait until morning when the sun will be behind us.'

'Bernard's coming out!' Alexandre shouts, pointing at the movement around *Tamata*'s stern. I watch Bernard as he moves along the pass, sitting in the front of his folding canoe and using only one paddle in true native fashion. I'm sure he understands our problem. He stops just inside the entrance of the pass and sits there holding his paddle vertically in the air – a guiding saviour silhouetted by the sparkling water, haloed by the setting sun.

'He's waiting to guide us in,' Anne says. Bernard remains motionless as I build up to maximum speed and head straight for him. Now my greatest concern is that I might run him down. On the final wave we pick up more speed and fly in fast. He scurries out of the way at the very last moment.

'Whoopee!' I scream to him in delight as we exchange huge smiles of mutual satisfaction. Soon we have our mooring organised and invite our visitors aboard, although I have the uneasy feeling that it's we who are the visitors.

Immediately Bernard says they were surprised not to find us here when they arrived a few days ago. They have a scheduled flight to Paris in the near future and therefore will not be able to stay long. I'm relieved.

The next morning we find Bernard ashore down a six-foot-deep hole. Using only a machete and an old paint can, he is digging us a well. His body is running wet with sweat as he scatters the sandy soil neatly and smoothly all around his hole. He has decided that this spot, close to the boat on the east side, is the ideal place to settle.

I glance at Anne and she reflects my anxiety. She knows I've already decided to look for a place on the west side of the atoll, far from the roar of the surf and sea spray, and not too far from the tank. Watching Bernard as he sweats on our behalf, I'm not sure how to react. I take Veronique aside and quietly explain we have things stored in the tank and we intend to unload the hens and our belongings on the other side of the island. Alexandre is caught by the idea that you can dig a hole in the sand and find fresh water. He wants to wait for the water to appear. Only by promising him faithfully that we'll come back later are we able to drag him away.

Mini-Mini's mast is set, the gaff mainsail raised, the leeboard attached, and the steering oar arranged in its place. Our empty water barrels from Ahe are already aboard. We add the floorboards, the roll of chicken wire, the large tarpaulin, some of the boxes of supplies, and the big axe and machete. We place the cage with the hens on top and take up our places for the crossing. Kiki is in front as our lookout, the children just behind on the front bench, the captain and first mate aft to operate the sail and steering oar. Dou-Dou, after searching all over the dinghy for a suitable place, settles herself on top of the hens' cage.

With the mainsail full, we wind our way across the lagoon in a zigzag course that wanders around the many coral heads that reach up to the surface. Boobies and frigate birds fly close by to look at the newest arrivals. A green turtle sticks his head up for a quick glance before he paddles out of our way. Alexandre and Anaïs cry out at each new discovery as they hang over the side of *Mini-Mini* and gaze at the branches of live coral and multitude of highly coloured tropical fish that pass below them. As a shark slides close by, the tension aboard mounts and we know we are back.

Our enjoyable cruise ends all too soon as we scratch abruptly to a stop on the far side of the lagoon. We tie *Mini-Mini* to the low bushes on the sandy beach and slowly begin to unload our belongings. Nearby a large, resting stingray flaps up a cloud of sand and moves to a quieter spot.

We begin by clearing away some of the mass of fallen fronds that have built up on the forest floor and arrange our things in the shade of the coconut trees to establish a sort of base camp. I attempt to cut a path directly through the thick undergrowth of the jungle to the tank, which lies about three hundred yards away, but soon give up. Instead, we take the longer but easier route around by the beach. Our supplies remain untouched and our note unread. A little water has collected in the children's arrangement of pots and pans. No papayas have sprouted.

Water is our first priority. Back at the base camp we attach the corners of our large tarpaulin to four convenient coconut trees, giving it a slope into the wind. At the lowest point we place a two-hundred-litre plastic container. Now even in a short shower we should collect a considerable amount of drinking water. One thing in our favour is that it's the end of September and the beginning of the wet season.

The mosquitoes soon prove to be a nuisance; Anne and the children burn piles of coconut leaves to keep them away.

'Come and help me make a run for the hens,' I call to Alexandre.

'A run so they can't run away,' he laughs.

Together we pick out another group of four coconut trees. Then I attach some rope about six feet off the ground. Anne joins us as we unroll the chicken mesh, attach it vertically to the now taut rope, and place pieces of coral around the base. For the door I simply overlap the ends. The hens are delighted with their freedom. They scratch and search for insects and take turns trying out the new perch. Anne collects and splits fresh sprouted coconuts for them.

Bernard and Veronique come to visit us around midday. Bernard has found water but is disappointed. 'It's very salty,' he says. He's going to start another hole farther away from the lagoon, which he assures us will be less salty.

For fresh food, the coconut crabs are the easiest to trap. Anne grills yet another one in the hot embers of her fire. There are so many young coconut trees here that the normally rare source of heart-of-palm begins to takes on the aspect of a weed choking up the plantation.

Already using woven coconut leaves for serving plates, Bernard insists on a half-coconut to hold his food. He even cuts himself a set of chopsticks from the hard wood of a nearby Miki-Miki bush. So far I have not reverted to this primitive state of the jungle native. In fact, I sit very comfortably in my aluminium folding chair and eat from a flat glass plate with a stainless steel fork and knife. My goal here is not to 'go primitive'. I came here primarily to isolate myself from human society, perhaps to search for the primitive in all things, but not necessarily to act out the life of the noble savage. I have no objection to using twentieth century materials, particularly those which have evolved to be simple and efficient and bring a minimum of interference to daily life. Indeed, in the challenging environment of the sea, I depend on the comfort and reliability of my fibreglass boat with its diesel motor. I appreciate the advantage of the light aluminium masts, the strong nylon and terylene lines and sails, coupled with the durable stainless steel rigging and fittings.

On an island, tools like a good axe and machete are indispensable. Plastic shoes protect our feet from the sharp coral. Glass dishes and cups, stainless steel utensils, even our stainless steel pressure cooker – all give simple and dependable service. I admit my folding chair is not necessary. It was a last-minute gift from a good friend. I sit here surrounded by untamed jungle, content to enjoy my present state of evolution, which is somewhere between the civilised radical and radical primitive.

Our shared picnic passes very agreeably. Veronique stays busy with her video camera, taking photos of our setting to support an article Bernard intends to write about his visit here for *Neptune Yachting* magazine. There is little I can say, but I fret that our newly discovered hideaway is to become the centrepiece of a popular yachting magazine.

It's late afternoon when we sail *Mini-Mini* back upwind to the boat. She's slow and takes her own time to make her way into the small choppy waves characteristic of an enclosed lagoon. We don't care. We have time; the most important thing is that we have begun.

'Look! Look!' Alexandre cries as we arrive next morning with another load of supplies. 'There are only three hens left, and the run is full of coconut crabs!' He's almost crying in his distress. I notice the other three hens not too far away.

'Don't worry,' I tell him. 'First we clear the crabs out, then we chase the hens in.' A total of seven large coconut crabs are entangled in the mesh of the run. It takes quite some time to extract them from the wire while all the time avoiding their dangerous pincers, which would break the bone of a caught finger. The hens are easier, and soon all six are safely back in the run. I take the extra precaution now of laying mesh over the top of the run.

'To keep the chickens in and the crabs out,' Alexandre explains to his attentive sister.

At midday, Bernard and Veronique tell us the second well is finished. The water is still salty. 'It must never rain here,' Bernard states. 'That's the only explanation for the high saltiness of the ground water.'

I hope he's wrong, but during our first 10-day visit here and our return, it's true, we have seen no rain. Speaking of rainfall leads the discussion to the water cistern. I explain the problem of the overhanging coconut tree to Bernard, knowing full well that coconut trees are his speciality. Bernard is enthusiastic to help. We make a rendezvous to cut the offending tree down early next morning. Later that afternoon, I build a high shelf between more coconut trees to store our belongings off the ground – then arrange a small tent over everything, just in case it rains!

The difficulty with the offending tree is that if we just cut it down, it will fall directly onto the tank, doing considerable damage. As a solution, I've now brought in my strongest anchor line, which we will attach to the tree in such a way that, as it falls, it will be pulled off to one side of the tank.

Bernard strips the bark from a young green tree and fixes a loop around his ankles. He carries several coils of anchor line over his shoulder and shows his expertise by doing a sort of hop-hop up the vertical trunk, locking his feet firmly around the tree after each hop. Halfway up the tree and about thirty feet from the ground, he attaches the line. We pull it tight and tie it around the bases of two other coconut trees.

Before leaving the boat this morning, I spent considerable time honing my best axe to what I considered a razor edge. Bernard, after running his thumb across the cutting edge, explains, 'Now, Ron, the axe has to be really sharp. The coconut tree is a very hard wood.' I worry about his thumb as he runs it once more along the sharp edge to reinforce his point. The coconut wood is indeed hard. We don't chop; rather we chip our way into its centre. Often the axe just bounces back without making any impression.

It requires teamwork. Anne and Veronique both take their turns. We break frequently for a drink of water. After twenty minutes, we begin to hear the first crick-cracks, which tell us the trunk is weakening. 'Back, back, back,' I warn the children with some urgency. 'Where's Kiki?' We stop cutting and call her, but the crick-cracking continues. Kiki doesn't appear, and our calls become a little desperate. Finally, she wanders back from her own exploration of the island. Anne quickly leads the children and dog even farther away from danger.

In slow motion the tree begins to topple. The rope takes the strain and squeals under the enormous weight. I'm afraid it may snap and disappear behind another coconut tree. With a final crack, a great swish of falling leaves and a resounding thump, our defeated giant crashes to the ground. It misses the tank by a few inches.

Encouraged by our success, we chop down other coconut trees close by the tank. Before the morning is over, looking straight up from the tank we can see a large area of clear blue sky.

The next day I begin work on the tank. I repair the walls and set in the new outlet pipe. When I finish, I give a light cement wash to all the outside walls. The total result is very pleasing. The walls are square and clean, and the tank has an air of newness about it. I print the date and our names alongside the shiny new brass tap and arrange our corrugated aluminium sheets to deliver any rainwater into the tank.

Bernard's comment that 'it must never rain here' is worrisome, but again I look at the thick vegetation. 'It must rain here sometime,' I say. 'We just have to be patient.'

'I hope our water outlasts our patience,' Anne is quick to reply.

As Bernard and Veronique prepare to leave, we stand by to help with the mooring lines. Black smoke rings fly from the vertical dry exhaust which sticks out of the cabin roof as he hand-cranks his rarely used air-cooled diesel motor to life, the sound of which reminds me of an old farm tractor. He hoists the mainsail, but it flaps uselessly in the light headwind. We shout 'goodbye,' 'good luck' and 'thank you' as they gather in their last line and head out of the pass to the open sea.

We're alone, and I take a long moment to breathe freely and enjoy this state that appears so difficult to achieve, despite our determination and passionate efforts. In general, I am supportive and sensitive to the needs of other people and their endeavours. Characters like Bernard fascinate me. However, when I have something important to do, I prefer to be alone and left to my own devices. Anne's presence doesn't really upset my daily routine. We seem to be able to work together as a good team, even though we each have a totally different way of doing things.

With this new-found peace I take a moment to assess our progress. In our enthusiasm and perhaps unsettled by our visitors, I note that we've been rushing. All our supplies and materials are ashore. We have arrived. Now we can do what we came here to do: take our time!

Our base camp, though, is not ideal. It's too close to the jungle; we can never hope to control all the invading mosquitoes, rats and coconut crabs. We need something smaller, more manageable and more isolated from the main jungle. I think perhaps one of the small islets just north of South Islet may be the answer.

7

We Find a Home

The mainsail dances in the fresh breeze as I hold *Mini-Mini*'s head into the wind. Kiki sits, as usual, up in the bow. The children are installed on their front bench. The steering oar is in position. 'Ready!' I shout.

'Okay, okay,' the children reply in happy unison, and I push off, jump aboard, slide the leeboard into position and grab the steering oar all in one practised and smooth movement. With a sharp tug on the mainsail sheet we're underway, heading north up the lagoon to search for a suitable islet home. We wave back to Anne, who stays on the beach ready to commence her fishing expedition for the morning.

We haven't gone far before our progress is stopped by a long strip of coral that appears to stretch fully across the lagoon.

'Try to find a pass,' I shout quickly to my lookouts.

'Over there!' Alexandre points to his immediate left. It's an opening, but it's narrow, shallow and shaped like an 'S'. Halfway through I'm obliged to jump overboard and bob along up to my neck in water. With some difficulty I manage to physically push *Mini-Mini* around the last bend while the soft coral crunches and gives way under my feet. Once clear of the pass, we make a short downwind run to a small attractive tree-covered islet. This is the first islet going north on this west side of the lagoon. We land gently on a small crescent-shaped beach of fine coral. A large group of frigate birds, perched low on the bushes, eyes us with suspicion.

Vultures, I think again as the children and Kiki hold back, afraid. I take a step forward and one frigate flaps his six-foot wing span and with some confusion takes off. Another follows. The majority just sit there staring down at us as though we are the advance parade of the newest circus in town. Two fairy terns swoop down over our heads to add to the confusion and excitement with their noise and chatter.

As unobtrusively as possible we stow the mainsail, secure Mini-Mini to a tree and slide by our staring spectators to step into obscurity under the cool shade of the shoreline trees. We push our way through the branches on our expedition of discovery until we reach a fairly large natural clearing. It's an area of clean coral on possibly the highest point of the islet. Surrounded by large green trees with round flat leaves and heavy foliage, it has a pleasant forest feeling, yet with an open airy atmosphere. This is how I imagined our ideal setting: a rustic jungle house resting peacefully in the centre of a clearing, surrounded by a fertile garden. The large trees would provide protection from strong winds, shade from the sun and a play area for the children where they would be safe from the danger of falling coconuts.

Alexandre joins my enthusiasm for this location by finding a branch suitable for a Tarzan swing. Then, together, the children find another branch suspended low over the ground. This they ride like a bucking bronco with regular wild whoops and squeals of delight.

We wander farther into the centre of this islet and enter

a cluster of about fifty coconut trees growing in a low circular area. I guess that sometime in the evolution of the island, this area had flooded during a storm, allowing coconuts from the main island to float in and take root. These trees are younger and lower than those on South Islet and bear healthier-looking coconuts. The centre of this low area also looks like a possible place for a well. Beyond the coconut trees stand other large green trees. More important, we find Nono trees which, enclosed by the thick jungle, have stretched long and straight toward the sky to find the light. They are perfect for building a house.

One or two rats scurry among the trees, but we see no coconut crabs. Back on the beach we talk about the mosquitoes.

'Did you get bitten?' I ask Alexandre.

'No,' he replies, taking a quick look at his hands and legs. 'How about you, Anaïs?'

'No, Pap,' she answers, copying Alexandre with a quick examination of her body.

'Me neither,' I say. 'Wow, no mosquitoes! Wait till we tell Mummy.'

Anne, back from a successful fishing trip, is burning leaves and being 'bitten to death' when we arrive and relate our happy no-mosquitoes story.

'That's not possible,' she says. 'There are mosquitoes, rats and crabs all over this island.'

'Well, we saw rats, but no mosquitoes and no coconut crabs,' I argue. 'It's an ideal little islet. There are coconut trees and good building wood.'

'And a super bouncing branch,' Alexandre adds in support.

The next day I'm back on the islet armed with my big axe, bushman's saw and machete. First, I'm faced with two old twisted trees that have struggled year after year to survive here. Since they lie right in the centre of my house plot, they have to go. I'm sad to end their long and continuous battle with life in only a few minutes. As does the head-chopping executioner before he does his thing, I beg their pardon.

For the other trees I need only to cut away their lower branches. The small bushes I uproot completely from the loose coral and sand, without too much difficulty. The odd straight Nono I clean off carefully and lay to one side. I'm so pleased to have at last started to establish our place that time ceases to exist. I work on hour after hour in an effortless passion.

At midday I take a rest on the beach to cool off in the lagoon. I realise my feet are hurting. On closer examination I find that my toes are swollen and have small bubble blisters all around my toenails; my small coral cuts are also red and painful. It can only be the ants! I noticed them around my feet during the morning, but I gave them little attention as they didn't appear to have a painful sting. Now I see that they have been systematically eating off all the soft or broken skin on my feet.

On my return I check out the ground more closely and find there are ants everywhere – an average of one ant to each square centimetre of ground area. But it's when I pull up roots and turn over large pieces of coral that I disturb their nests and they flow over my feet en masse.

When I return to the boat in the evening, I bathe my feet in hot sterilised water and explain to Anne that maybe the ants could be a problem.

'I can't wait to see this marvellous islet,' she says. 'No mosquitoes, but millions of flesh-eating ants. Wonderful!'

'Hopefully, as we clear, they'll disappear,' I counter. 'For the moment I suggest we defend ourselves by wearing socks.'

When we arrive together the next morning, Anne is fortunately impressed with the little clearing I've made. After an initial critical examination she becomes enthusiastic and agrees that this islet looks manageable and suitable for a settlement. We organise a storage shelf and small kitchen under the shade of the large trees. Nobody mentions mosquitoes, rats or ants. I begin to feel I've overreacted, being the only one wearing socks. Soon the children are brushing ants off their feet. They head out for the open beach. Anne's feet are red, but she says nothing. Her principles tend to lean more toward those of Bernard than mine do. For her, real natives don't wear socks! I can only imagine that her lack of complaining is based on the same principle. Real natives who don't wear socks don't complain either! At midday, without comment, we join the children on the ant-free beach to eat our meal.

We relax in the shade as the day continues on to its warmest hour after noontime, which rarely rises above ninety degrees. The coolest time is in the early hours of the morning. Then it may drop to as low as seventy degrees. The temperature here is strictly controlled by the surrounding ocean, which remains constant at around seventy degrees. Any heating of the air by the hot tropical sun is quickly moderated by this vigilant controller.

It is within this narrow range of warmth that we pace ourselves. We live largely without clothes. In places of privacy in the tropics, most people find that clothes serve only to restrict airflow and promote irritation and sweating in sensitive areas. We simply adopt this comfortable and healthy habit ashore.

But the tropical sun also causes skin cancer. Fortunately, in our nudity, we are protected by the thick foliage of the trees – provided we remain under cover. When we must be exposed to the sun while sailing in the lagoon or walking on the open reef or beaches, we cover up as much as possible. The children wear light pyjamas, we wear our flour-sack uniforms. We all wear Anne's coconut-leaf hats. We also wear this gear on expeditions to mosquito-infested areas.

Like the Polynesians who live on the atolls, we adopt, if possible, the habit of tackling heavy physical outdoor work when the sun is low in the sky: first light in the morning or late afternoon.

We are completely comfortable with our healthy nudity habit as are many of our friends within the tropical sailing community. If outside company arrives, we dress appropriately. We feel so natural totally nude it takes a real effort to wear clothes.

The children, for no reason I can think of, named our South Islet base camp Puti-Puti, doubling the name in the Polynesian way, as in Bora-Bora. We need a name for our new islet. We start with Anne, Anaïs, Alexandre, and don't forget the Ants. It has to begin with A. A becomes An, then Ana, and finally, in true Polynesian style again, we end up with Ana-Ana.

Anne, who enjoys sailing *Mini-Mini* around the lagoon for her fishing trips, now volunteers to transfer all our belongings from the base camp to Ana-Ana, leaving me free to concentrate on building the house. She has also decided that fishing, which we shared on Ahe, is to be totally her thing here. As for the other daily chores like cooking and tending the children, we will share these as usual.

We are all excited about getting started. Ana-Ana is to be our islet to organise as we wish, making paths through the trees, clearing a large area for the house, planting out a garden and digging a well. Most importantly, like the Nomadic Terns, we have settled to build our nest and now go about our preparations with a concentrated contentment and feeling of well-being. The work is largely physical and sometimes exhausting if under the overhead sun. As with making love, passion dominates the physical effort. We smile often to communicate our mutual pleasure as our paths cross during the day.

My collected pile of Nono trees grows fast. They are plentiful, exceptionally straight and so conveniently placed close to the house that I can't believe our good fortune. Very soon I have the first large main frame fixed together and laid out on the ground. Needing help, I call out to Anne, 'Come help me raise this frame to the vertical position.'

Despite our valiant but fumbling attempts, the foundation frame of our new house remains firmly on the ground. 'It's too heavy,' Anne states, and in a way she's right. The wood is green, but also the frame is tall, thin and very wobbly. We try again, using forked props to raise it fairly high off the ground. We reach that point where we have to drop the props, physically take one leg each and just push. We begin a circus act of two very serious, hardworking clowns carrying out a risky task. I can easily imagine audience cries of 'Wooooo!' and 'Ahaaaa!' accompanying our frantic efforts to raise this wobbly frame high in the sky. We make desperate gestures to each other between Anne's repeated statements of 'It's going to fall!' Only we have no appreciative audience and Anne is definitely not seeing the funny side of our difficulties.

Now comes the climax, when she has to balance the frame vertical and alone while I attach a support. Her reaction is predictably pessimistic, and the historic raising of the first foundations of the newest society dedicated to the search for man's place in the universe is marred by loud outbursts of 'I can't hold it!' and 'It's falling!' As usual, however, despite her expressions to the contrary, Anne is extremely capable and cool. The first frame now stands upright and proud in anticipation of its pivotal role. The other two main frames, although raised with similar ceremony, are less trouble. It's not long before the complete box skeleton of a house stands solid and tall in the centre of our clearing.

I take my time to carefully set the several salvaged two-by-four floor beams flat and level over the Nono frames. Finally the moment arrives when I can lay down my precious clean white floorboards. Not only is it a luxury to walk and lie down on this raised clean flat platform, it also brings back fond memories of my Scottish childhood when each year for the local 'Highland Gathering' the village erected a high stage for the dancing and piping competitions. It was always a time of intense excitement when we children would play being 'on stage', and once up there would generally dance around and act the fool. All too often the game would develop into warfare, where those 'up here' would fight to retain their supremacy over those 'down there'. Now once again I feel that special and important status of being one of those 'up here'.

The ants are also impressed with the new structure and are not beyond the 'get up there' mentality. They swarm up the legs and wander all over the new floor in a concentrated effort to join the ruling classes. For her own reasons, Anne is playing down the presence and nuisance of the ants. For me, there is no way I am going to pass my nights sleeping blissfully and dreaming my dreams while ants eat out my transcended body from the toes up.

With the zinc we found on Puti-Puti, a dash of Scottish engineering genius, and some trial and error, I make nine small circular troughs that I attach tightly around each leg of the main house frames. I seal the joints and fill each trough with old engine oil. The brave-hearted ants make some determined attempts to storm the defensive moats by piling their bodies up across the oil. It doesn't work and eventually they are forced to accept defeat and leave the enterprising lord in peace to fully enjoy the sanctuary of his established castle.

For the roof, I lay on all the aluminium sheets and use the roll of zinc to cover the ridge and to form a water gutter on both sides that will lead every last drop of rainwater down into our awaiting containers. When I've finished, I lie down on the floor to admire my masterpiece, only to see all the corroded pinholes in the aluminium sheets light up like Van Gogh's *Starry Night*. Using the last of the boat's waterproof sealing paste, I carefully fill in each hole until all of these little bright shining suns in my universe revert to black holes.

We've been here for three weeks by this stage, and it hasn't rained. The house has a roof and floor but still no walls. We decide to take a chance and move ashore with our mattresses and bedding. Although it will be so much easier from the work point of view to sleep on Ana-Ana, I'm going to miss our daily sails across the lagoon. The return in the evening after a hard physical day is the most enjoyable. The sun is low, and the seabirds cry out to us as they return from their day spent way out at sea. Anne usually takes the helm and sails as close to the wind as possible. We talk about our day: all the fish Mum caught and how Anaïs cut her knee again, Alexandre's new hut in the trees, the bottles we've found, the shells we've collected and the progress in the building of the house. Often we sing our favourite song:

> Or would you like to swing on a star,
> carry moonbeams home in a jar,
> and be better off than you are.
> Or would you rather be a mule?
> A mule is an animal with . . .

The coral heads we've passed twice each day are now familiar, as are the names and positions of the surrounding islets. Even the local sharks now know our routine and more or less leave us alone. Still, we didn't come to the island to live on a boat. Our real adventure is just beginning.

8

Rain and Pain

Once installed ashore, we find we're pleased with the luxury of so much extra space and spread our mattresses out across the bare floor in anticipation of a peaceful night. The parakeets, on land for the first time, rest quietly as the tropical twilight quickly changes into darkness. The children, exhausted after their active day, are soon sound asleep. Anne and I are awake, sensitive to the touch of the light cool air on our now relaxed naked bodies. The quiet hiss of coconut leaves whispers secrets from our new surroundings. Mingled with the rumble of distant surf, they produce a soothing background lullaby for lovers.

Then we hear another sound – pit-pat-ping, pit-pat-ping. It's raining.

Quickly we hang up the tarpaulin on the windward wall and slide the children's beds into the centre of the floor. As the rain slowly increases, we concentrate on positioning our containers to catch every last drop of the fresh water that now flows freely from both gutters. The downpour continues and we hang up a sheet on the other wall to try to keep at least one corner of the house dry. The children sleep on, their bliss undisturbed by the pouring rain and intruding dampness of the night.

Wet and nude in the pitch dark, we struggle and concentrate to guide the precious stream of life-giving pure water into the containers. We're soaked, chilled and delighted all at the same time. Aided by flashlight, we watch each container fill up until it overflows. We soon collect over seven hundred litres, enough for several weeks' supply. The rain continues. We return to bed, enjoy a triumphant midnight cuddle, then rest quietly together in warm comfort. We eventually fall asleep to the satisfying sound of fresh water freely overflowing from our full containers.

In the morning it's still raining. The tops of the short choppy waves break off and their white caps run down the lagoon like a stampede of wild horses. The surrounding trees protect us from the worst of the gale. From time to time an occasional gust arrives to billow out the tarpaulin and sheet and to rock the house's flimsy structure. Alexandre and Anaïs dance naked under the steady waterfall from each gutter. They become passionate about filling up everything and anything that will hold water: bottles, the kettle, pans, cups, jars and half coconuts. It's so long since our barrels have been used. Anne uses this luxury of running water to wash out each full container and then fill them up again.

Lighting the morning fire is a little difficult. With a piece of corrugated aluminium I create enough protection to boil the kettle and heat the frying pan for crepes. For breakfast we find a dry and comfortable place under the house where we settle to enjoy our usual breakfast of muesli and fresh yoghurt. We finish with warm fresh crepes and honey as we sip our hot coffee and peep out at the dripping jungle. We repeat over and over, with giggles and grins, Bernard's prediction, 'It must never rain on Caroline.'

Our fresh yoghurt comes from a 'starter' available from chemists and sealed in a small packet. We warm a litre of milk (powdered mixed with water) using the finger method to determine the desired temperature (if you can't keep your finger immersed it's too hot!), then add the starter and leave the mixture covered, away from the wind, for about ten hours. We then have one litre of fresh yoghurt! Without refrigeration it must be remade each day with another litre of warmed milk, adding this time a few spoonfuls of the previous day's batch. It's delicious and a healthy addition to our diet. Our muesli we mix ourselves using oats or various grains as a base, then adding peanuts, sunflower seeds, raisins, dates and prunes. Using Anne's old hand coffee grinder, we grind our coffee from whole coffee beans.

Now that we have enough water and everything is clean, we would like the rain to stop and the blue skies and gentle wind to return. It's not to be. If anything, the local conditions have deteriorated. One dangerous thing about coral atolls is that they are very vulnerable in storm conditions. Extremely low barometric pressure, as, for example, near the centre of a cyclone, coupled with a storm surge can raise the surrounding sea level by as much as ten feet. At that point the high storm waves can easily run across the flat barrier reef and totally sweep over the low islets. On the coral banks by the seaside of Ana-Ana it's possible to see the clearly marked steps that indicate the height of the breakers from previous storms that have formed this islet. In severe storm conditions an islet can be washed away completely.

The basin on Ana-Ana where the coconut trees grow is only eighteen inches above high-water level and is now beginning to fill up. The site where the house stands is a mere six feet above sea level. 'We could get a cyclone,' Anne states anxiously.

'We're outside the normal cyclone area,' I remind her one more time; we've had this conversation before. 'Here we're ten degrees south of the equator. Cyclones start in these latitudes but then head off south before they gather strength.'

'So, we could get one here,' she insists.

'The last recorded cyclone here was in 1878. That's over one hundred years ago. It would be just too bad if we had a cyclone in our first month here.'

There is no conclusion to this conversation, so I leave to check out *Mini-Mini* on the beach. The normal tide range here is less than two feet. I see that the water level in the lagoon is already well above the highest tide mark and our little beach is completely flooded. It's also blocked up with pieces of wood and debris washed over from the islands to the east. *Mini-Mini* is safe enough, but for extra security I heave her a little higher up the beach. She's heavy with water and I struggle for some time in the loose coral before I'm satisfied.

On the way back to the house my stomach feels a little odd. Then it begins to hurt. I imagine all the worst possibilities. A pulled muscle, stomach cramps, a hernia or maybe even a ruptured appendix. I lie down for a moment's rest, hoping it will go away, but soon I can feel the house sway so badly that I have to return outside and attach ropes from the ridge to the nearby trees. When I finish, Anne tells me I'm as white as the sheet that hangs on the wall. It's true I feel a little light-headed. My stomach is solid to touch and now aches badly.

We brought a medical book with us called *Where There Is No Doctor*. It's especially prepared for isolated or Third World communities and covers explicitly, with the aid of many weird diagrams, most common medical problems. Anne now searches out all the stomach complaints from cancer to worms and finally focuses on appendicitis. She probes my stomach looking for tender spots and has me lifting my legs as directed by the book. She finds nothing conclusive. In my pain all I want is to be left alone.

She knows that if I have a real problem her situation is quite serious. She can sail and navigate the boat sufficiently, but knows little about the engine or electrical system. She also knows that at this moment the main battery cable on the boat is disconnected to prevent electrical leakage. Soon she's back with a notebook and wants me to describe in exact detail how to reconnect the cable to the battery.

'And the engine?' she asks, and continues to take notes as I lie in pain and misery, working my way through the starting procedure of the motor. Finally, preoccupied with her new information, she leaves me in peace to continue her chores of the day. I now imagine how she discusses her present situation with the children: 'Now if Daddy dies, this is what we do.'

Although I'm anxious and in pain, I'm really not too deeply worried. In general, most of my aches and pains, when left alone and given a little rest, disappear. I am more upset about the hold-up in my work program. As the day passes, I fast and stay in bed. Everything is wet and an air of damp depression settles in with the night. I can't sleep and lie quiet, listening hour after hour to the rain hammering on the roof. Despite the howling of the wind in the trees I can hear the rising thunder of the surf all around the islet. As I reach that stage of being very quiet and clear, I focus on the thought of being dead. I imagine I no longer exist as a living person – heart stopped, no thoughts, nothing, cold, stiff, dead. I even imagine the reactions of my family.

I fall asleep sometime before dawn and stay in bed all the next day. I continue to eat nothing, and slowly the painful ache eases. The second night I sleep better. Next morning the pain is gone, the rain has stopped, the wind has dropped and the sun is shining. I wander around Ana-Ana as if I've been away for a long holiday. I still feel a little weak, but whatever it was has passed. For Anne, though, it has definitely not passed.

'If it was your appendix,' she states angrily, 'we have to leave right now!'

'It's gone,' I argue. 'We've only just arrived. The house is looking really good, the hens are thriving, we're making good progress. I'm ready to start the garden. We can't just leave.'

'You don't know what you had, but you're ready to take the chance that it might happen again. I don't find that funny,' she protests.

'Okay, okay,' I concede, 'tonight we'll go back to the boat. I'll try to contact Les on the radio and we'll get some medical advice.'

The Pacific Maritime Network begins at six o'clock local Caroline time. It's an amazing net that covers the whole Pacific basin from America across to Australia. Hundreds of ham radio operators, on land and at sea, tune in every evening to the same frequency, all with the possibility of contributing to the net by simply pressing their transmit buttons. It's like the Internet. Besides the locally organised coffee klatch, the subjects covered are everything from weather information, the daily position of boats on passage, connections from a yacht's radio to family on shore by phone, a full emergency service for any boat in distress, and a medical emergency service. It's all organised by the radio amateur enthusiasts themselves, and it's free.

What we're looking for is medical advice. I let the radio warm up awhile and fine-tune the antenna. Tonight it's Fred from Hawaii who is in control. I wait for a space, then transmit my call sign.

'Ron, how are things on Caroline?' Fred replies, bright and breezy. We haven't been very active on the radio recently with all the work ashore, but Fred helped us during our search for *Marara* and knows we are here.

'I'm looking for Les, Fred. Can I give him a call?'

'Yes, go ahead.'

'I'm in here, Ron.' I hear Les's deep voice slip in during the pause.

'Les, it's good to hear you. We've a little problem here and need some medical advice.'

'Stand by, Ron. I'll call Doctor John in New Zealand.'

Doctor John replies on the second call. Les repeats all our call signs and informs the net that we're moving to another frequency. I add a quick 'thanks' to Fred. It's all taken less than five minutes, and now I'm in direct contact with a qualified doctor in New Zealand. I relate all my symptoms to Doctor John: the location, duration and intensity of the pain.

'Just tell me it's not appendicitis,' I finish, quickly glancing at Anne.

'Well, don't worry, Ron,' he says immediately. 'It's not your appendix. It sounds to me more like a case of acute indigestion that has now passed.' He talks slowly and reassuringly.

'That's all I wanted to hear, Doctor John.' I smile at Anne. 'And thank you very much for being there.'

I chat with Les awhile and bring him up to date on the state of the house and our storm. I promise to give him a call when I eventually bring the radio ashore. Anne says little more but appears more relaxed now that she won't have to face the intricacies of the boat's electrical system and diesel motor alone.

Daily I bake bread, or make crepes, and we eat at regular times. The hens and animals are fed at the same hour. As in music, a rhythm begins to appear in our routine, which with repetition becomes a familiar and comfortable melody that moves us steadily along, in tune with our surroundings. We are strong in our island environment. Any forces that threaten our survival are slight and more or less predictable.

For navigation we carried aboard a quartz watch because correct time is all-important for taking sun or star sights. For our radio schedules we use this same watch. For our daily routine on Caroline all we need to use is the sun. In the tropics this is not difficult to do. Sunrise is at six am. At twelve noon the sun is directly overhead. At nine o'clock in the morning the sun is halfway between the east horizon and overhead. In fact, it isn't difficult to split the ninety-degree angle between horizon and overhead into six equal parts (hours) and guess the time to within an accuracy of fifteen minutes.

Telling the time by the moon at night is a little more complicated, but once one is familiar with the daily changing phases of the moon and their relationship with the sun, it is possible. For example, the new moon, the first slither of crescent, always appears at sunset (about fifteen degrees, or one hour, above the west horizon) and therefore sets at seven pm. The next day, because of its progression of one hour per day, at sunset it appears thirty degrees above the horizon and sets at eight pm. The half moon is overhead at sunset and can be used like the sun for marking six hours until it sets in the west. The full moon rises as the sun sets at six pm and can be used, similarly to the sun, to find the time right through the night. The tides tie in with the moon and provide another point of reference for the general progress of time.

The phases of the moon have strong effects on nature. For example, at a certain stage of the moon occurring once monthly, all the land crabs come up out of the ground to wander freely around together in the open areas. We relish the feeling of being sensitive to and moving alongside this natural sequence of events.

9

Our World on Ana-Ana

It may once have been easy to believe that this planet, with everything on it, was put here solely for the benefit of mankind, to use or abuse as we pleased. Faced as we are with more and more life-threatening pollution, compounded by scientific information about the evolution of our universe and other universes, this belief, like the one that the world was flat, is no longer credible.

Often I compare our millions of Ana-Ana ants, who know only this islet as their universe, to the human race. They, like us, are limited in their capabilities. In time they may explore some of the other islets of Caroline, but they will never be able to cross the wide space of the Pacific Ocean to discover the whole of this planet. Our islet is Earth. We make the odd ambitious journey of discovery from time to time, but in the end we have to admit that we are restricted to our little islet. Compared to Ana-Ana's ants we have incredible knowledge. Nevertheless, we have similar difficulties obtaining information about the mysteries of the great outside universe. We, like the ants, have to come to terms with our immediate surroundings.

Restricted as we are to new scientific understanding, we can still make logical guesses about what's going on around us. Practical scientific knowledge should calm our fears and keep us away from superstitious beliefs or the temptation simply to adopt mythological explanations for our day-to-day mysteries. And here, in our own little kingdom, we can try to live a life that is more attuned to the laws of nature.

We are fairly distant here from the dreams and ambitions of other human beings. Yet we must never forget that we share this planet with others who, stimulated by the characteristics of the original creative force, are driven by opportunist and expansionist ideas. For the moment we hold on to that rare luxury called space and freedom, but for how long?

On Caroline so far, we have escaped the meddling megalomaniacs. Here we have only the aggressive sharks, persistent coconut crabs, bloodthirsty mosquitoes and flesh-eating ants. We also have a dreamer who is now faced with a real philosophical problem: whether to build a wheelbarrow or not. I have found a suitable round fishing buoy with a hole through the middle for a wheel. I have an aluminium axle, complete with bearings, from the self-steering unit of *Petrel*. Since I already use *Mini-Mini* as water transport, why not create a wheelbarrow to transport things on land? I ask myself. But didn't the whole Industrial Revolution start with the wheel, which then rolled us all into subversion? Yet since the force of life is creative, ever-producing and expanding, perhaps we will feel fundamentally more in tune with it when we ourselves are also expanding, creating and producing. We still need to take time to use our wonderful capacity for logic to consider the direction of our constant quest for progress.

The animals don't appear to be as prone as we are to blunder onward towards restless, passionate 'progress'. Nor do they live in contented bliss and harmony. They appear to accept their natural way of life more calmly than we do.

We could learn a lot by observing their ability to humbly do their thing, shake off the nasties and settle for the odd moment of sexual stimulation.

Today, human beings on this same planet who have reached a comparable stage of evolution live entirely different day-to-day lives. Some remain deep in a jungle of one kind or another, while others pass their lives in insulated, sterile buildings with buttons to control all that surrounds them.

Here, in isolation on Caroline, I imagine that we have some freedom of choice, some quality control. But do we? I wonder to what extent our conditioning dominates our daily decisions and actions? It seems to me that the great variety of belief systems in our world reveals their ultimate potential for flexibility. Culture and education are, after all, only the general adoption, by a group, of certain patterns and beliefs that have developed within that group and eventually established themselves. We all passionately defend our personal mentality and beliefs, not because of their concrete certainty, but precisely because they are fragile and transitory. They represent our reality, our sincere efforts to make sense of the complex confusion that comes from being alive. All of these conjectures keep me amused as I contemplate the basis on which we established our own alternative lifestyle on this isolated island. I put the decision about the progressive wheelbarrow on standby for the moment, not because I have come to any great conclusion but because of lack of time. I have a house to finish.

We must begin the pressing and earnest physical search for coconut leaves for our sleeping hut that has no walls. I've made large hanging shutters that, when fixed open, will give extra shade around the house and allow air to flow freely through our sleeping quarters. To cover the shutters, I need lots and lots of woven coconut leaves.

Anne is the weaving specialist. On Ahe, with the help of Mama Fana, she learned how to make mats, plates, baskets, hats and roof and wall coverings, all from weaving the plentiful coconut leaves. First we collect the fallen and mature brown coconut leaves from the forest floor, trim off the heavy ends and soak the leaves overnight in the sea. Salting, the Polynesians say, preserves the leaves. Then, as we pull apart the two small end leaves, the centre stalk neatly splits down the middle. Each half-leaf is then woven by laying every second long strand back and over, under, its neighbour. Finally, the two woven half-leaves are laid one on top of the other and attached at both ends. The result is a fairly solid leaf around seven feet long by two feet wide. In one day, working for about three hours, Anne prepares no more than ten leaves. I need a total of three hundred leaves. It's a slow rhythm: the leaves grow to maturity, fall, are gathered up, woven, then fixed to the shutters to form our sanctuary.

It's difficult to think about creating anything that resembles a normal garden here on Ana-Ana. The whole islet is made up of loose pieces of coral, with only a sandy soil in between. I dig holes in the coral rubble and use a box sieve to separate out the little soil. It's slow and tiring work. As I reach the end of my row of holes, I have collected a meagre pile of poor, sandy soil. 'Come on,' I say to the children. 'We're going on a ground hunt.'

Around the base of some old trees by the beach we find a thin black layer of humus created from years of decomposing fallen leaves. This we scrape up carefully with our spoons. After half an hour's work we fill only half of our communal bucket. Anaïs wanders off looking for something more interesting to do, and Alexandre says he's tired of this work. It's not encouraging. I reread my book on hydroponics.

On Canton Atoll, closer than we are to the equator, an American military base existed for a while. They built a hydroponics farm to produce all their fresh vegetables. It's an interesting possibility which I consider for some time. In the end, though, I come down on the side of the primitives, Bernard and Anne. The mixing of chemicals I can leave to the laboratory specialists.

Omer once planned to start a garden here. He told me he had shipped in sacks of good volcanic soil from Tahiti to Caroline, then dumped this soil in a pile somewhere close to the tank on South Islet. The next day, searching deep under a group of pandanus trees, I find his imported gold dust. The soil still looks good, although it soon becomes evident that over the years the local roots have been warring for possession of this rich treasure. Locked in fixed battle positions, they fully occupy this precious territory. My intrusion is not appreciated and they attempt to reject all my efforts to steal their hard-won land. Any contact with the surrounding mass of razor-sharp pandanus leaves results in long weeping scratches on my exposed skin. The mosquitoes are thick too. Before I am finally driven away, I have claimed some booty: three half-sacks of fertile Tahiti ground.

Back at our patch I make my holes smaller. I fill them with a mix of dead leaves, sandy soil, humus and the imported soil. My dream is first to create a forest of papaya trees – then I'll settle for a plantation of tomatoes, sweet potatoes, green beans, watermelons and Chinese cabbage.

October arrives, and we take a break to celebrate the three birthdays that fall within four days. Alexandre is four, Anaïs two, and Anne adds another year to her fast disappearing youth. We plan an expedition to the *Petrel*. Despite its relative closeness to the pass and boat, Anne and the children have never visited it.

There's something basic about beachcombing and

treasure-hunting that bypasses all our polite patterns of social behaviour. Beachcombing touches the dark and profound depths of our basic nature. Isolated on islands, I've seen many instances where friends suddenly turn enemies over a bit of valueless debris that has floated onto the beach. The battle that ensues is above ethics and belongs more to the jungle code: when you find something, it's yours – provided you can hold on to it. Here for the moment we are king and queen, prince and princess – everything in our kingdom is ours. We have little motivation for conflict. After a quick look over the stranded *Petrel*, Anne and the children lose interest in my potential building materials and possible valuable stainless-steel fittings. They continue a little further on to check out the more interesting mess of Gary's camping area.

I remain with *Petrel* and first unscrew the formica salon table. This respectable table is destined to become the centrepiece for Caroline's proposed nursery school. I continue to remove all the plywood panels and useful pieces of wood. I ignore the expensive stainless-steel fittings but concentrate on the aluminium mast. This I intend to use to support my shore-based radio antenna.

A little later I find Anne and the children happily sifting through the rubbish dump of Gary's personal belongings. Sails, ropes, the broken self-steering unit, a miniature television set, clothes, shoes, plates, forks and spoons lie scattered around among the coconut trees. Alexandre has found a cup, Anaïs a hairbrush, an egg box and a small pan. A dozen beer bottles stand together under a coconut tree and Anne wonders if Gary wisely drank one each night, or went on a depressive drinking binge. We load up the dinghy and place the salvaged aluminium mast on top. We're grossly overloaded with little room left for the crew. Crossing the lagoon, we have a few bad moments as we manoeuvre our tiny cargo ship back to Ana-Ana.

We've all had a good day, and even though the children have received only modest birthday presents, they go to bed highly excited with all their newly found treasures laid out alongside their mattresses. When the children are soundly asleep, Anne produces one of our six bottles of special occasion wine. It's a moment of reflection. A little drunk, we indulge in nostalgic memories of our romantic love affair that has taken us on our long journey from Sark to Caroline.

Only once we were underway did Anne slowly divulge our progressive drift away from Europe to her anxious parents. We danced in delight on deck amid the neon lights of Lisbon harbour. We swam in warm fresh water far up the River Tage, explored the sights and pub-crawled in Madeira, boogied to the reggae bands in Barbados. Alexandre was conceived amid the drama of penetrating the Panama Canal. Crossing the Pacific had been difficult because – perhaps due to El Niño – the trade winds that year failed completely. We were seventy-two days at sea, either struggling to make progress in the squalls, or more or less motionless in the water with the spinnaker limply wrapped around the shrouds.

We recall the bliss of arriving at the dark mountains of the Marquesas Islands. Giving birth to Alexandre wasn't easy for Anne. Her labour pains started at midnight while we were on the boat in the tiny marina of Rangiroa. We walked, with frequent stops, the two miles to the small hospital clinic. The facilities there were minimal, and a temporary military doctor was in charge. Fortunately, Alexandre made his exit without too many complications, although we had some anxious moments when the placenta refused to leave the security of the womb to face extinction in the outside world. Anaïs was more easily delivered in a modern clinic in downtown Papeete. We have lived together for five years, twenty-four hours a day, sharing love, joy, our children and all our daily trials and tribulations. We are a complete family on a special adventure.

A little tipsy, we congratulate ourselves on our two healthy children. The wine done, hand in hand we make our way to bed. Once there, we muffle our giggles as we celebrate our love in stifled silence. Our peaceful birthday children sleep on in their own state of bliss.

The next day, stimulated perhaps by the after-effects of alcohol, I have an idea that will make cooking easier. I presume that when man matured to the upright walking position he gave some serious thought to how to do his cooking standing up – or if he didn't, he should have. To make our stove, I start with a circular wall of pieces of flat coral, then fill in the centre with rubble. On top I place our metal cooking frame over what is now a conveniently placed waist-high fire. 'Very civilised,' Anne cannot resist commenting as she questions the philosophical purity of my activities.

'It's to go with your stainless-steel pressure cooker and your cast-iron crepe pan,' I return defensively.

'If you're not careful, you'll organise us back into a totally computer-dominated, high-tech way of life,' she teases.

'Don't worry about the practical improvements,' I assure her. 'My real obsession is that of a prophet who wants to create a new and radical religion which really comes to terms with all that is gloriously beautiful yet tragically sad in our world.'

'There are many books on that subject, written by great minds. What can you hope to add?' I've heard stuff like this from her before.

'I question everything, that's all. I want to see things for myself. After years of observation and chasing endless possible paths through the channels of my mind, I have to reach some sort of overall conclusions. I want to share them.' Anne lets the matter drop as we return to our first priority: practical survival.

Our fresh drinking water has to be managed carefully. Already we wash our dishes and pans in the lagoon. We use salt water for all the steam cooking in the pressure cooker. Now, instead of adding salt when making bread, rice or soups, we simply use a mix of one-third pure seawater to two-thirds fresh water. By adding salt water to our food during cooking, we reap the benefit of absorbing all the many minerals and trace elements that exist in seawater and are missing in our collected rainwater.

Well water is our other possible source of relatively clean water to wash with. I start digging at the lowest level of the basin where the coconut trees grow. When only eighteen inches down, I hit water. 'You were lucky,' Anne says, remembering Bernard's hard work on his deep holes.

'I'm Scottish,' I say with a smug smile.

After sampling my source, we have to agree that it smells. Now begins another long discussion about the comparative saltiness of our well on Ahe, Bernard's two wells by the pass, and this one. The only real conclusion is that they are all a better source of washing-up water than the sea. My well does indeed stink of sulphur, but I remember reading some- where that ground water found in the Northern Cook Islands had been analysed and found comparable to the popular healing spa waters of Harrogate, in England.

The local rats are another source of concern. They have multiplied to such an extent that, as they come around each evening to finish off the hen's split coconuts, I can count five to ten rats crawling over each half-coconut. I can hear hundreds of them rush back into the forest as I approach the hen run in the darkness. They have also installed them- selves in the roof of the hen run and started to build nests in the woven layers of coconut leaves of our house and kitchen.

Aided by the children, I build a medium-sized square cage, and then at one end incorporate a tunnel with a balanced trapdoor. 'Now, if we put lots of fresh coconut into the cage, what happens?' I ask my attentive and curious helpers.

'The rats smell the food, search for the tunnel, go through the trapdoor and are caught!' Alexandre is pleased to explain, while Anaïs puts her hand through the trap door and gets it stuck, demonstrating the effectiveness of the whole device.

That night, we set the trap by the hen run and sit quietly not far away. From time to time I turn on the torch. There are rats all over the cage; some have found the way in, while those left outside become ever more desperate to join those feasting inside. 'It's working good,' Alexandre whispers in the darkness.

In the morning, Dou-Dou, who makes her odd brave contribution to rat control, tries to put her paw through the mesh and into the cage full of captives. Kiki simply stares arrogantly at the panicked prisoners. As still as a statue she stands, her nose an inch from the mesh.

As I immerse the cage into the sea to quickly drown the caught marauders, I watch for the reaction of the children. They show little distress at the fate of the enemy; their real interest is in the feeding of the sharks. One by one, I throw the drowned rats into the shallows between Ana-Ana and Puti-Puti. The ever-present sharks move in, racing each other to fight aggressively over each tasty morsel. We watch, tense, as a total of forty-three rats disappear forever between rows of jagged teeth. I pass on our rat-trapping success to our regular radio friends. From then on the 'rat count' becomes an established topic of discussion.

The rats are always there, multiplying as quickly as I can

catch them. I have a concentrated purge from time to time for around ten days to reduce their numbers. Within a few weeks they increase, and I have to begin exterminating them again. If they stay around the hen house, they are little trouble. Nesting in the house, however, they are annoying, the squeak-squeak of feeding babies disturbing our sleep. We keep all our food in solid sealed containers so it is never at risk.

Most days Anne goes fishing, often in the pass, sometimes in the lagoon or out on the open reef. Usually her catch is good, but we always have to exercise a certain amount of caution. There's a kind of algae that grows on broken coral which, when eaten by the fish, makes them poisonous. Different fish in different lagoons are affected, and there's no way to tell which fish are poisonous except by trial and error. If enough of this poison is absorbed into the body, you become ill with symptoms comparable to a really bad flu, with aching joints and loss of power in the muscles. There is no cure. It passes, but your body remains supersensitive to even the slightest amount of this poison for up to one year.

I had an idea to use the trapped rats to test which fish are poisonous. But some experts told Anne that rats have a high resistance to what is known as ciguatera poisoning. They added that cats have about the same sensitivity as humans. Here we have very little broken coral and don't really expect to find any of this poison. Nevertheless, as Anne catches each new type of fish she immediately feeds a tiny piece to our laboratory cat – not enough to make her really ill but enough that we can notice symptoms. Fortunately for Dou-Dou, we have so far found no trace of poisoning. I don't like using Dou-Dou in this way, but here on the island our priorities are clear. If one of us humans is out of commission, everyone's life suffers, even Dou-Dou's.

Our days differ, but each morning you will find four nude bodies squatting out over the dry reef that borders the lagoon. With some trial and error we all decided that the silky leaves of the Tournefortia tree are the most suitable for toilet paper. For a while I worried about polluting the clean waters of the lagoon. I didn't know then about the 'sergeant majors'. These small striped fish wait in anticipation of our arrival, regular as clockwork, then fight desperately amongst themselves to clean up every last scrap.

Often, squatting there pensive and fully exposed, I wonder if any satellite observation teams are watching us on their high-definition monitors. Supposing they make systematic checks on these uninhabited islands for military purposes, surely they would notice our yacht permanently moored in the pass, and the shining aluminium roof of our house. Somehow it pleases me to imagine these observers locked up in their concrete bunkers hour after hour, analysing and reporting what they see on their screens, while we sit outside, warmed by the first rays of the morning sun, and feel the cool fresh breeze on our exposed skin. If by some chance they have found us, I hope that our carefree daily toilet activities bring a smile and little sunshine into their dark underground lives.

The day I install our solar panels, our little isolated community joins the space age. It's not without a feeling of grace that I watch our one hundred-ampere lead acid battery bubbling contentedly at midday as the charging rate from the panels rests steadily at ten amps. Now I can bring the transceiver radio ashore. For the antenna I raise *Petrel*'s thirty-foot mast on the highest bank of Ana-Ana and stay it to the nearby bushes. For another attachment point I throw a line over a forty-foot-high tree close to the house. I then raise my three-hundred-foot-long wire from the house to the mast. For a good ground I bury the last of my rolls of zinc.

Ham radio operators spend at least fifty per cent of their time talking about antennas and signal reports. Now I can properly join the club.

'You're pushing my signal needle past its maximum, Ron,' Les tells me with some surprise on the morning after my installation. 'What have you done?'

I explain my new shore-bound long wire arrangement and receive similar good reports from all the other operators on the net. This creates another problem. My strong signal now stimulates ham operators all around the world, who try to make contact with the rare isolated operator on Caroline Atoll. The contacts are always interesting. The problem is they want confirmation (QSL) cards for their collections. I have to explain that is a little difficult since we have no postal service.

Our other piece of electrical sophistication is the installation of two adjustable reading lights over the bed. The children, after their active day, need little encouragement to fall asleep. Nevertheless, Anne can now read them a short story before their eyes close. Our night-lights also give us the opportunity to indulge in that almost forgotten luxury of reading in bed.

Books are important in our isolation. With a good story we can escape to other worlds far from our practical daily routine and feet-on-the-ground existence. Often we enter into our stories so much that our breakfast conversation consists only of sharing the latest chapter of our current book. Anne's taste in books tends to be on the heavy side. When we left France she brought along her personal collection of books by Proust, Victor Hugo, Sartre, Rousseau and other serious authors. In general my reading material over the years has come from book swaps with other yachts or from tourist hotel libraries.

In such swaps, any John Le Carré story was always

pounced on as a treasure, as was any tale of true adventure. It's difficult to be too choosy with this source of popular books, but occasionally a special one turns up. Richard Bach's *Jonathan Livingston Seagull* caught me by surprise. I flew high page by page with this pure free spirit, to finish in tears of empathy. I rode alongside Robert M. Pirsig throughout his *Zen and the Art of Motorcycle Maintenance*, as he made his long physical journey across America on a BMW in search of himself, truth and the fundamental principle behind western civilised thought. Henry David Thoreau's *On the Duty of Civil Disobedience* gave me more food for thought than his better-known *Walden*. I had another surprise with Joseph Campbell's views on *The Power of Myth*, and found myself nodding along in agreement with his refreshingly clear thinking. The other book which set me thinking was *Albert Einstein: The Man and His Theories* by Hilaire Cuny. Here was a master of pure logic who nevertheless remained a dreamer when it came to the motivations of human nature.

Our other amusement is music. Anne plays a little guitar and occasionally brings it out to pass the time of day. In Scotland I played drums regularly at the village dances or dinner dances in the hotels. During the building of *Fleur d'Ecosse* this was my sole source of income. But drums and a small boat don't go together. For a while after leaving Scotland I messed around with a guitar tuned to an open chord. My missing fingers on the vital left hand limited any hopes of becoming a virtuoso, however. Then, in New Zealand, I came across an autoharp. This is an instrument based on the old European zither. With thirty-six strings it's basically a mini-harp. What makes it 'auto' is the attachment of a device whereby at the push of a simple button (as on an accordion) when strummed, it produces a full chord. Pushing buttons was something my left hand could

Fleur d'Ecosse, glass fibre construction, 28-feet long, covered-in cockpit, wishbone ketch rig. This faithful little boat sailed over 50,000 nautical miles before delivering us safely to our destination – Caroline Atoll.

Anne, city girl turned hunter and gatherer. When confronted, these coconut crabs tend to freeze so are easily caught and are good to eat. Their huge vice-like claws are strong enough to break a finger.

Anne with parrotfish speared on the reef. Primitive gypsy fishing girl, she eventually claimed Caroline's throne as queen of the island.

First camp on Ana-Ana. With driftwood shelves, table and benches, we begin to establish a stable routine of preparing meals at regular hours.

Two contented children enjoying their before-bedtime bath.
Alexandre has a cut-down plastic barrel, Anaïs a normal
galvanised bucket.

First frames of the
No-No house
with raised floor
made of flat pine
planks brought all
the way from
Tahiti.

Aluminium rain-catching roof, woven coconut leaves on the gables, rustic
balustrade around the floor – we have a sleeping house.

The kitchen: coconut leaf roof, fine coral floor, driftwood shelves, table, benches and washing-up area with suspended net to dry dishes.

Ron, the radical primitive, fixing one of Anne's woven coconut leaves from the large lifting shutters that provide walls for the house.

Settlement: sleeping house, kitchen, solar panels in the foreground and hanging wire mesh for drying bananas.

Making arrowroot flour: squeezing the grated tubers under running water to ease out the flour. When settled, the water is poured off and the fine flour dried out in the sun.

Amateur radio transceiver used for emergencies, medical advice and cyclone warnings. As for our connection with the outside world: we followed the news just in case of a nuclear war.

George, another loner, was our first visitor. He brought with him much needed supplies and food. *Sheila*, on the last leg of a circumnavigation, is even smaller than *Fleur d'Ecosse*.

Family of four on the steps of the finished house. Photo courtesy of George.

Fully protected from the burning sun, the children are ready for an expedition of beachcombing. Anne made the coconut hats; plastic sandals protect their feet against sharp coral.

Using the power of the wind to drive the sails and a tiny grinder, our windmill helped us make fine flour from whole wheat grains.

Cooking a typical fish meal using the new barbecue decorated with bottles brought up from the beach.

The biologists (from left to right): Kay, John, Anne, Alve, Anne of Caroline, captain Graham, Ron. It was Kay's passion to protect Caroline that ultimately led to our final troubles.

handle. The autoharp became my instrument. Over the years I learned various techniques for strumming and plucking, and I enjoyed endless hours of entertainment as I put together familiar songs and their chords. Years later I would earn my living playing this same instrument in the tourist hotels of Polynesia.

Our other morning preoccupation is with developments in the all-important garden. This can become quite involved as we try to outdo each other with details.

'Did you notice that two of the tomato flowers have fertilised?' Anne will start in a mood of fresh discovery.

'Yes,' I say, 'and some of the papaya trees are showing male and female flowers.'

'Also,' she says, 'I can find no tubers forming on the sweet potatoes.'

'Yes, I checked that too – lots of leaves, but no tubers.'

And so it continues. As it is for the ants, Ana-Ana has become our world, our whole universe: the garden is our captured territory; the house, our nest; this little family, an entire population. We remain highly conscious of our special exclusive world. We also know that we are not alone on this planet. Each day's joys are therefore treasured for their special moment of completeness.

10

An Interdependent Community

The initial excitement of settling in on our own coral island is gradually replaced by the solid comfort of our established routine. The pure, dreamlike quality of our independence is counterbalanced by the seriousness of the day-to-day decisions that ensure our survival. Each day the reality of these choices confronts us with a certain tension amid the peacefulness of our life on Caroline – even when the matter at hand is as small as a newborn chick.

Omer, our growing cock, now crows and wakes us each morning with his own sense of self-importance. The five hens have also been named. Moulin is red. Paris is grey. Venus has a white star under her ear. Lisa, who always seems excited, reminds us of an American girl who married a young local boy on Ahe. Rere, resembling a cock, has the Tahitian name for a male with female characteristics. In our anxiety for new chicks we applaud Omer each time he succeeds in mounting a hen.

The young hens have started laying, and both Rere and Lisa are brooding. Anne rearranges all the eggs so that each mother has ten eggs. I add a stepped stairway down from each nest. Then the morning arrives when the first small 'cheep-cheep!' ends our anticipation. 'Come and see!' I call excitedly to the children. Alexandre and Anaïs watch transfixed as a small hole appears in one egg. The chick then takes its first deep breath and the shell breaks open.

'They can walk straightaway,' I explain, 'and cry "cheep-cheep" for their mummy to notice them.'

'I can see three,' Alexandre says. 'They're hiding from us.'

'They're delicate for the first few days,' I tell him, 'and want to stay warm under their mummy.'

'First eggs, then chickens,' Anaïs observes philosophically and sits down to await further developments.

'There are five now,' Alexandre reports before long.

'I see some more,' Anaïs adds, not to be outdone. By the end of the day Rere has nine chicks, and the next morning Lisa has five. We're delighted, but as we watch the chicks move around the yard, somehow they seem unsure on their feet.

'Maybe first chicks are always a little weak,' I suggest as I note Anne's concern.

'Or maybe their diet is incomplete,' she adds, searching for some justification.

Next day we leave for an expedition to the cistern on Puti-Puti. During the rains this holding tank filled up considerably, then slowly but surely the water drained away again. I suspect there is a porous area at the very bottom of the tank. I'm becoming a little disillusioned with this tank; plus, I have no more cement. As a last effort I try to seal off the worst areas with the little remaining fibreglass and resin that I keep on the boat for emergencies. Anne uses her time to collect sacks of coconuts and mature brown coconut leaves. At the end of the afternoon *Mini-Mini*, heavily loaded, ploughs her way slowly back to Ana-Ana. We're all tired. Anaïs sleeps among the leaves.

We're still unloading on the beach when Alexandre comes running back from the house. 'All the chicks are dead!' he shouts. 'All of them, they're all dead!' We follow him quickly, and he shows us dead chicks lying around the hen run.

Anne starts crying. They were her babies, our first new life on Ana-Ana and our hope for the future. She won't stop crying and finally leaves the house to be alone out on the reef. I try to find an explanation for their deaths, but the only thing I come up with is that our hens are carrying some sort of virus or sickness.

I cook up some semolina for the children, give them their evening wash and put them to bed. It's quiet and dark when Anne returns. She's depressed. 'I'm fed up here,' she begins. She doesn't talk about the chicks – instead, she focuses on our other problem. 'We're running out of supplies,' she says. 'I shopped for only six months. We lost time in Ahe, and then you were feeding our supplies to the hens. I didn't calculate for that. If we intend to stay here another three months till the end of the cyclone season, we have to start rationing, now!'

I'm too tired to analyse anything more today. 'Tomorrow,' I say as we hold hands and let companionship and sleep ease our minds.

In the morning we've all calmed down. It's warm, the wind rustles the coconut leaves and the rising sun starts a fresh new day. Rere has three chicks; Lisa has one. Now I take time to examine the remaining chicks more carefully. They all have the same problem – their feet. Their toes have been attacked. 'It's the ants,' I say. 'They've eaten the tender flesh around their toenails as they did with us. For day-old chicks it was too much!'

All the remaining chicks, despite the handicap of having short stumpy toes and no toenails, somehow survive. That same day I build a special ant-free breeding cage on the same principle as the house. Each leg sits in a tin of engine oil. Now, at least, future chicks will have some time to mature and toughen up their skin before they face the killer ants on the open ground.

Christmas arrives. I build the children a smart driftwood car with steering and plastic buoys for wheels.

'Straight from no wheels to the evolution of the car,' Anne comments. 'You're just not a serious back-to-nature freak!'

'It's feet-driven like the Flintstones' car,' I humour the purity of her noble savage self-image. 'Non-polluting, non-killing and allowable.'

As for rules and regulations, we tend not to impose any on the children, nor to discipline them severely. Sensing the importance and obvious seriousness of our day-to-day situation, they contribute if they can or sensibly stay out of the way.

With the constant activity of the cock around the house they are also clear in their minds about matters of a sexual nature. Our nudity they accept as completely normal. Although Anne and I are discreet in our lovemaking, on a small boat or one-room sleeping house total privacy is impossible. We treat the children as the young adults they are, and always try to answer their questions honestly in a straightforward way. In general, they have a very close relationship with each other and appear to have an endless ability to create new amusements for themselves. Being naturally of a good disposition, they remain content.

There's much joy in our togetherness on Caroline. Sometimes I feel as though Anne and I are holding hands and flying. We're unable to hide from each other behind style, dress, social conventions or other people – we have no choice except to be real in all our tiredness or fear, physical pain or sadness. Having assumed total responsibility for our lives, we're a tiny interdependent community, relying on ourselves and each other rather than on 'experts' such as doctors, lawyers, lenders, engineers or teachers. If everyone on earth took such responsibility for themselves, I think to myself, the world would be a healthier place.

With life pared down to its essentials, special moments stand out. On Ahe, when both children were babies, each night I would take them in my arms and walk way out on the reef until they fell asleep. I remember Anaïs had a fixation with the moon and as soon as we were outside would twist and turn around in my arms until she found it. 'La lune! La lune!' she would then cry, and I would share this moment of discovery and the innocent wonder of a young child.

The new year begins with Anne dividing up our supplies, first into three-month parts, then each part into four-week parts, then each weekly part into seven-day parts. When she has finished, our ration for one day is one tin of vegetables or fruit, plus one cupful of either rice, couscous, lentils, dried beans or noodles. The one tin and cup are divided into three meals. Each meal is divided into four platefuls. The final individual portions are, needless to say, small! 'We have to depend on the island food to survive,' I insist, 'and simply rely less on our bought stores.'

Perhaps after a few years, we could adequately modify our diets and produce enough food to be self-sufficient on Caroline. It would mean adjusting to living without milk, butter, cooking oil, wheat, beans and brown rice as well as increasing the amount of fruit and vegetables from the garden and eggs from the hens. For now, we are obliged to harvest what we can from the land and sea.

We start with the heart-of-palm – it's abundant and full of vitamins. We add it to every meal. We eat it fresh; we boil it with rice. When fried, it tastes like mushrooms. We fill up on the spongy centres of coconuts that have lain on the ground until they sprouted. This the Polynesians call 'uto' and we cook it for an hour to make it digestible. We also grate the meaty coconut and squeeze out its rich oily milk. This all-purpose sauce can be added to almost anything.

Each day Anne supplies us with fish, crab, octopus or shellfish. Mostly it's adequate, but our high-protein meals leave us hungry. Once more we fill up by chewing on coconut meat. We supplement this with a weed called purslane, which is rich in vitamin C. We gather it easily along the beach. It's succulent like a salad, although fairly tasteless.

I've stopped making bread and crepes. Now I mix the little flour we have left with an equal amount of grated coconut. With some sugar added they bake up into tasty and filling coconut biscuits. Even so, our existing flour will last only two more weeks. We have the garden, but the papaya trees need a few more months before they will provide their first fruit. Fortunately, the tomatoes are fruiting and the long green beans are plentiful.

Strangely enough, we have plenty of energy and seem in excellent health. No one is carrying any extra fat, except maybe Anaïs, who still has her baby's belly. I keep assuring myself that we're not starving, or even nearly starving, and that the constantly hollow and empty feeling deep in my stomach comes only from a lack of solid starchy food. We could leave, except that, since we are bang in the middle of the cyclone season, we could be caught in a storm. Another possibility is to contact a passing yacht en route from either Hawaii to Tahiti or from the Marquesas to Tonga, as both routes pass reasonably close to Caroline. Then again, it's the cyclone season and cruising yachts normally don't begin to sail until March. We try to put our hardships aside and get on with our routine. Then another source of ongoing irritation comes to a head.

Right from the start I have refused to let Anne interfere with the design or construction of any of my building projects. 'It's my art,' I defend myself in an attempt to clarify my seeming paranoia, 'and the only way I can find satisfaction in creating anything is to do it my way. It's my passion – and each personal success gives me the motivation to go on and do other things.'

'And my ways?' Anne argues, bristling.

'You're working out your fishing technique in your own way. I don't interfere with your general routine and habits.' I refrain from mentioning that, although I think a fish trap would be a more efficient way of securing our daily protein, her hook-and-line method gives her so much pleasure that I wouldn't dream of suggesting a trap at this point. 'We both leave the children free to play in their own fashion,' I add. She thinks about this.

'Life is art in action,' I continue in the manner of a Sunday church sermon, 'and, like making love, it's very personal, humble and honest. Any outside interference, organisation or intellectualising makes it less satisfying.'

'It takes two to make love,' she says coyly and quickly.

'Exactly,' I say, 'that's my point: making love is two individuals doing their own sexy thing. With true compassion and understanding, both can be satisfied.'

She frowns but is silent.

My independent efforts continue as I build a smart decorative balustrade around the square house floor. The entrance opening is adorned by a stairway of wide driftwood steps. In each corner of the house I attach shelves with a small table underneath. We choose our corners to arrange our personal belongings. The children have their own books, drawing materials and their own collection of shells and feathers. Anne neatly stacks all her books together, then her jewellery, then her precious small glass balls and shell collection. In my corner I keep some of my books and arrange a permanent place for all my small tools, glues, fishing gear and flashlight. The transceiver radio totally fills the fourth corner to become our miniature radio shack.

We have no furniture except the table from *Petrel*. Our mattresses remain spread out on the floor. We always have clean sheets and refrain from eating in the house so as not to attract cockroaches and lizards. My final touch is to nail a fancy carved plaque by the door. 'No-No', it reads, named after the wood we used and the no-no we are saying to the outside world.

Having no flour is annoying, especially when I know that in the Cook Islands the islanders still grow arrowroot and extract its floury starch. Since wild arrowroot grows here on Caroline, one day we set off to South Islet to try our hand at the business of starch production.

After passing a full morning digging and scraping in the hard-packed sand and coral, we fill only one bucket with small arrowroot tubers. Back at the house we peel these tough tubers and finely grate them into a basin. By placing the gratings on a stretched cotton cloth we can pour water over them and systematically squeeze out the starch. The fine starch turns the water cloudy. After the starch eventually settles on the bottom of the basin, we carefully pour the water off. The snow-white residue of pure starch that remains on the bottom is put to dry in the sun. It all takes time. Three mornings' work finally produces only one small bowlful of starch, enough for one baking of coconut biscuits.

'Too difficult,' Anne comments, and I can't disagree. The starch production is put aside. I redirect my available energy into the building of a kitchen.

The structure is of mixed design between an A-frame and a normal pitched roof. Coconut leaves are laid over the roof frames. The floor area is raked clear and covered with fine coral. I add shelves for storage and work areas; then from driftwood I construct a proper eating table and two long benches. One of *Petrel*'s plywood panels is used to hold a sunken basin to form a washing-up area, and a net is suspended over the top to wind-dry the dishes. To complete the buildings and provide total comfort, I construct a roof over the raised coral barbecue area. Again using gathered driftwood, I add benches on either side to create work areas or to use as beds alongside the fire in the cool of the evening.

Although we have become better and better organised, I have found no solution to the lack of garden soil. One day I head off alone up the lagoon on a new expedition in search of earth. On Pig Islet, which lies just over one mile across the lagoon, I've noticed that there is a small but solid forest of large *Pisonia Grandis* trees like those I encountered on Vostok. As I enter the forest it's evident that there are many more birds here, their chirping and chattering totally filling this enclosed green cathedral. It's another world within this already exotic and strangely spiritual island. Immediately I become sensitive to the embrace and closeness of the pulsing life that surrounds me, to the point where I feel as though it is entering every cell of my body. For a long time I am unable to move, captivated by this warm, sensual and strangely erotic ambience. The intense feeling passes and I find, as on Vostok, that I'm standing on a thick spongy layer of black humus. It's soft and easy to collect. Composed of years of rotten leaves and bird droppings, this soil must be rich. Soon I've filled up all twelve of the sacks I've brought along.

Mini-Mini lies heavily loaded in the water. It's calm in the lee of the islet and the wind is light. I drift and dream my way back across the lagoon with the same feeling of contentment and well-being that follows intense lovemaking.

PART TWO

Progress and Reflections

11

A Helpful Stranger Comes to Call

March arrives and we're still on food rationing. Les is on the radio. 'Ron, some yachts have just arrived in the Marquesas. If you still need supplies, why don't you give them a call?'

'Will do, Les.' I put out a general call to the Marquesas. One yacht answers. They tell me they are heading direct to Tahiti, but will ask around the yachts in the anchorage for anyone coming our way. Two days later a single-handed Australian, George, joins the net.

'George, this is Ron. I'm living on a deserted island six hundred miles west of the Marquesas.'

'You're living alone on a desert island?'

'No, I'm not alone. I have my wife and two young children. We've been here six months and we're running a little low on supplies. Is there any chance of you coming this way?'

'Well, yes, I'm heading your way, but it's the last stage of my circumnavigation. My plan was to sail more or less direct to Brisbane.'

'Yes, I can understand that, George, but we need a little shopping. Could you possibly swing by here on your way? You wouldn't even have to stop over. I could meet you on the lee side of the island, pick up the supplies and you'd be on your way.'

George is not overenthusiastic. He takes time to explain that his boat is only twenty-five feet long. He would have to exchange more of his money to buy our stores, and how is he going to be repaid? Plus he knows coral islands, being low on the horizon, are dangerous and difficult to find. He would have to do extra navigation.

I tell him our island is a little special, and, if he wishes, we could get him in through the pass, where he could rest up for a few days as our guest. Also, I tell him I hold a supply of American dollars for payment.

'Well, I would like to help,' he says eventually. 'I'll have to think about it.'

Two days later George is back on the radio. He says, 'Okay, I'll do what I can.'

We compose and send a much modified and reduced shopping list, as we are afraid our original quantities would make him change his mind. Ordering supplies on amateur radio is not done, since that is considered commercial. Ham radio is strictly a social hobby. Under the circumstances, however, when I pass on our list to George, nobody complains.

25 kg of rice – a small sack
25 kg of flour – a half sack from the bakery
2 kg of sugar – 2 packs
11 kg of powdered milk – 6 big cans
6 kg lentils – 12 packets

George copies our list carefully and without comment. 'Thanks, George,' I say sincerely and with some relief. 'Give us a call when you leave the Marquesas and I'll bring the VHF ashore and keep it on standby.'

With this short communication a new atmosphere of excitement enters our lives. Not only do we have food coming, after six months we're going to have our first visitor – someone who is a stranger to us. Anne brings out her collection of small shells that the Polynesians use to make necklaces. Now she punches two little holes in each shell and, with the help of the children, threads them onto nylon fishing line.

On Caroline there are no frangipani or the Tiare de Tahiti flowers that the Polynesians use to make welcoming and farewell necklaces. We explain this deficiency to the children. The day after, they arrive back at the house with a basket full of orange-coloured blossoms that they have found by themselves on the local *Cordia* trees. They immediately begin to make flower necklaces.

'You have to make them on the day he arrives,' I explain, 'so they'll be fresh.'

'That's okay,' Alexandre says, 'we'll make more then.'

Having found a game with a purpose, they now spend hours and hours collecting and threading their fresh blossoms onto thin nylon thread, until every day our nudity is adorned with orange blossom necklaces.

Each day George is our main topic of conversation. Will he want to stay? Will the pass be open? Will he sleep ashore? Should we try to catch lobsters for him the night before he arrives? Will he think to bring fresh fruit, or even plants? And, finally, since he's bringing more food, can we ease up on rationing now?

I begin to view our settlement through the eyes of a visitor. I decide it's a bit of a mess. Cut branches, bushes and small uprooted trees still lie around from our first clearing. A small mountain of used coconut husks has built up close to the kitchen. Piling all the cut wood and coconuts together, I make huge fires that burn all day and continue well into the dark night. 'Don't worry,' I tell our satellite observers, 'we're just clearing up.'

Using a wide board, I hammer in a line of six-inch nails to make a large rake. This I use to clear away the larger pieces of coral to leave a respectable path of fine coral from the beach to the house and from the house to the well. I erect a discreet wall of coconut leaves around our open shower area. I remind Anne that George may be shocked by her total nudity and she should consider this during his stay.

One morning after the radio net has finished, I announce, 'George has left the Marquesas.' The excitement over the imminent arrival of our visitor increases and becomes totally out of all proportion to the event itself. After all, he is just a passing yachtsman who has been kind enough to help us out. But we've been alone and private here for six months. It's a dramatic development for someone to enter our exclusive, isolated world. Even our sleep is disturbed, as if in anticipation of a special royal guest.

After six days of absolute silence, the VHF bursts into life: 'Caroline Island, Caroline Island, this is yacht *Sheila*, yacht *Sheila* calling Caroline Island.'

'George, this is Ron. I have good copy. Where exactly are you?' We remain on channel sixteen, normally strictly reserved as a calling channel. I am fairly sure there are no other ships within hundreds of miles of the island.

'I'm just off the north end of the island. I estimate I should be by the pass in a little over one hour.'

'Okay, okay, understood, George. Wait for me by the pass. I'm on my way. I'll come out to meet you in the dinghy.'

'Roger, roger. I'll see you soon.'

I run around in a final fury of organisation, straightening bottles, picking up leaves and pulling the bedcovers smooth. As I sweep the floor one last time, I have the strong sensation of being a suburban housewife. 'Just keep everything tidy until I get back,' I shout to the children as I head off to the beach.

The inflatable dinghy makes slow progress as I row across

the lagoon against the wind. When I reach the pass, I see *Sheila*. She's a small sailboat, but being such an unusual sight close to the island, she looks strangely large and unreal. A strong outgoing current propels me fast through the pass entrance to arrive directly into the turbulent open ocean. The dinghy feels small, and I am obliged to continue to row out a considerable distance offshore as George is reluctant to approach too close in to the reef. Alongside *Sheila* I pass up the oars and quickly jump aboard; then I tie the dinghy off the stern.

'Good fellow, you've brought some banana plants,' I say as we shake hands. George is solidly built, middle aged, and has a correctness of manner that reminds me of Omer Darr.

'Well, they've been drenched a few times by the sea,' he apologises. 'I do hope they will survive.'

'The pass is not possible right now,' I explain immediately. 'There's a strong outgoing current that will remain until dark. What I suggest we do is head around to the lee side of the island for the night. If the weather holds, we'll get you in in the morning.'

'That sounds fine to me, Ron – you're the local pilot.'

On George's VHF I explain our plan to Anne. When we arrive behind Ana-Ana, everyone, including Kiki and Dou-Dou, is down at the edge of the reef to see the visitor. I have a chance to point out 'who's who' to George before they wave us goodbye and leave us to our night at sea.

Hove-to, *Sheila* is comfortable, and we slowly crab our way sideways along the coast in calm conditions. I rest pleasantly on watch in the cockpit while George makes us a snack below. We share our meal with the sunset, then talk until it's quite dark. George is tired, and when I suggest that I will be fine keeping watch until around midnight, he goes straight to bed.

The almost-full moon is already high. My head is busy

from all our talk. We're so insular here that it's difficult to feel any real involvement with the outside world. An earth-quake in California, a change of government in India or a general election in Great Britain – all share about the same passing news value. The only thing that could affect our situation is perhaps an all-out nuclear war. For that one reason alone, I make an effort to follow world news and monitor the east-west temperature. On the other hand, it's important to me to see how George, the outsider, will react to our style of life here. Will he see it as a great personal search for absolutes and ideals, or will he focus on other, simpler, more practical aspects?

Earlier, when we waved goodnight to Anne and the children, I could easily visualise how we might look to visitors on a cruise ship. As my watch passes, I let my thoughts run on, until I imagine myself as the informed guide talking to his group of multinational tourists: 'And here we have a family who have decided to live in isolation from modern society. They have developed their own special mini-culture and value system and, in general, make the minimum impact on their environment and surround-ings. They consider their super-logic no more unusual than the birds do their wings, a special gift that allows them to survive in their own particular way. Their sense of progress is no more than an awareness of the blossoms that come and go on the trees. Their home is a temporary shelter. Although they have no formal religion, they are motivated by the deep sense of their own spirituality.'

I dream on for a long time in this manner. We humans are funny creatures who pass our lives trying to achieve so many glorious ideals, far removed from the miracle of simply being ourselves. Is it pure arrogance for us to try to prove our superiority on this planet? Are we just carried along by the popular, commercially oriented mass culture? Or are we motivated by the combination of our personal ability to dream and fulfil our ideals? Are we so desperate to leave some lasting individual mark to prove that we once lived? Or is it pure fear that drives us to find more security? Could it be a desire for power and status within the group? Or perhaps we are driven by the desire to satisfy our well-developed sexual appetites.

What madness is it that builds pyramids, constructs skyscrapers and massacres millions of people in the name of an ideal? Are we really the victims and helpless pawns of some hazardous universal force that unthinkingly pulls things together before leaving them to survive, with little or no thought about what the outcome might be? Whatever drives us doesn't appear to be good, balanced common sense.

Often I sit on the beach of this beautiful, rich island and experience the joy of being at one with everything. I look into the clear lagoon with all the colourful tropical fish. I look at the birds, and all that surrounds me. I experience the pleasure of being a family sharing the ups and downs of each day, the satisfaction of drinking fresh clean water and eating good natural food. In moments like these I have the strong sensation, in my bones, that the super-developed section of the human race has, for whatever reason, sold itself terribly short.

I return to my present joy of being alone in the cockpit of this small boat and continue to cruise up and down the coast until sometime after midnight. I give up when my eyes refuse to stay open. I call George and quickly retire below to the warm familiar womb of comfort in a snug bunk, aboard a small sailboat.

After a morning mug of steaming hot coffee, I question George on the power and reliability of his engine. We can navigate the pass, I assure him, but we don't want any mechanical problems. George, anxious by nature, is well prepared and organised, and says he has full confidence in his boat and motor. Just the same, my questions have made him nervous. As we approach the pass, I can see he's worried.

'It looks worse than it is,' I repeat, to try to calm his anxiety. 'The conditions are all in our favour.'

George accepts my explanation, but with the entrance close by and the pass looking very small indeed among the breaking waves, he is definitely not happy.

'Just do exactly what I say,' I assure him, 'and we'll make it.'

He gives me one last hard questioning look, then braves his fear to head his precious home and source of transport in toward the small menacing entrance to Blind Passage.

Quietly I continue my regular instructions to position his boat exactly at the middle of the entrance. As we arrive, the last wave lifts us up and over to the left side. 'It's all right,' I say again. 'Turn right a little.' The boat begins to surf and we enter fast. In his excitement, he's overcorrected. We fly into the pass much too close to the northern edge of the solid coral reef. I'm afraid to whoop my customary cowboy call of relief for fear it may convince George that I'm totally out of my mind.

It's only later, when we become more familiar, that George confides his feelings to me. 'Entering that pass is probably the most dangerous thing that I have ever done in my whole life,' he says seriously. That, coming from someone who has just sailed alone around the world, gives me cause to wonder if indeed I have begun to lose my sense of perspective.

'How do you feel about outboard motors?' he asks when we finish tying up *Sheila* alongside *Fleur d'Ecosse*.

'Well, for us it's a real pleasure to live without them,' I tell him sincerely, 'but it's a bit of a row across the lagoon. It's as you like, George; we're just so pleased to have our supplies.'

His small outboard remains quietly strapped aboard while we row the two supply-laden inflatables peacefully side by side across the lagoon. We discuss the birds, the clear water, the live coral and the fishing. Eventually, George states, 'I have to say, Ron, you've picked a real nice spot to live.' It's a fine compliment from this worldwide sailor.

The children meet us on the beach. They hesitate shyly, holding their shell necklaces along with today's fresh orange blossom necklaces. 'Put them around his neck and give him a kiss on each cheek,' Anne instructs them. She is more or less covered up by a flimsy sarong, wearing nothing underneath. George is down on his knees in front of the children, and with some fumbling and lots of giggling, the welcoming ceremony is completed. As we walk together along the clean path up to the house, it's my turn to be tense. What I've done here is so private, so personal, I'm not sure I want it to be reduced to any kind of showpiece.

Fortunately the children take over: 'This is where we sleep, this is where we eat. Look! We now have a roof over the fire. We wash with the water from the well, it smells. That's Omer, there's Moulin. The parakeets fight; that's why they stay separated. Dou-Dou wants to eat the parakeets. That's Kiki – she catches fish out on the reef.' They show him the garden and the hen house and explain the problem with the chicks and the ants. Back in the house, Anne goes through all the details about the hens and tells George of our disappointment with the first chicks. I'm surprised at her intensity and how strongly she remains affected by this memory.

Anaïs then appears with one of the surviving toeless chicks to show to George. Now I'm beginning to feel a little sorry for George, still tired from his voyage, having to listen to all our domestic dramas after six months of solitude. Fortunately, being single-handed, he's pleased with the company and seems to be enjoying himself. Eventually he says, 'I just can't believe you've created all this on your own in only six months.'

Soon Anne leaves for her morning fishing trip. George is happy to rest awhile ashore. For my part, I'm pleased to share my daily routine. Together we prepare and bake our first bread in two months. Later, as we all sit around a table of fresh fish, tomatoes, watermelon, our first cucumber and heart-of-palm salad – the best local produce that Caroline can offer to our special guest – I make a toast: 'To our royal visitor and first local hero, King George.'

Anne tries to stay covered up. More often than not, though, she forgets and struts around the place naked, no more conscious of her nudity than the dog or the children. If George is shocked, he doesn't show it.

George's visit coincides with Easter. Anne sacrifices five potential breeding eggs for the children to decorate. Then I watch, once more amazed by the adaptability of this city girl who has cast off more than her bra. She takes Rere by the feet and chops off her head. Blood sprays over her bare legs. 'She's not a good layer or a good mother,' she explains earnestly. Roasted, Rere is also tough and not very tasty. For us it's a special treat to take a break from fish and more fish. I'm not sure George fully shares our delight in the change of diet.

After a stay of twelve days, George announces that his visit has been one of the greatest experiences of his whole circumnavigation. 'I'm so pleased I called,' he finishes, 'and sorry I didn't bring you more supplies.'

'No problem, George,' I reply. 'Thanks to you we now have enough food to get by, and we really appreciate your generous efforts on our behalf and having your company.' Our goodbyes are completed by the children, who come in with more kisses and the ritual flower necklaces.

We help him prepare to exit the pass. Since it's relatively calm, he has no difficulties leaving. We sail back across the lagoon pensive and left a little at a loss by his sudden departure. Back at our house, though, there are things to be done and we quickly pick up our roles and settle back into our old familiar routine.

Fortunately, one of the banana plants he brought has survived its salt-showered journey. Long after he has gone this plant will produce our first bananas. These, along with the regular supply of bananas produced from offspring plants, are always referred to as 'George's bananas'.

More than bananas continue to remind us of our first visitor, who came as a stranger and left as our friend. George not only brought us essential supplies for our existence, but his very presence brought us an additional perspective and understanding of our grand adventure in solitude.

12

The End of Our First Year

As memories of George's visit fade with the passing days, our lives are given over once again to the ebb and flow of our routines and adventures. I turn my attention to our faithful local transport.

Mini-Mini, with only her modest mainsail, is generally slow and cannot sail very close to the wind. With material from one of *Petrel's* sails I sew her up a new jib sail. Now, with a fresh breeze and if we're not overloaded, I can plane across the lagoon at twelve knots like a racing dinghy. Fully loaded, we can maintain three to four knots even against the wind. With this new improvement in power we all leave on an expedition up to the north of the island.

The lagoon is calm, the breeze moderate. Finding a passage through the maze of coral takes time, but even with these deviations we need no more than two hours to sail the six miles up the lagoon. We trail a small plastic octopus on a double hook behind the boat. Halfway up the lagoon we are rewarded with a large jack fish. Our lunch is assured.

On arrival, I show Anne and the children the 'flying saucer site'. It doesn't really look like it's been used for a very long time. Just the same, the mere thought of some kind of extraterrestrial prowling around at night on the island gives us a creepy feeling. We move away quickly from its spooky vibrations to the open beach.

Our interest is beachcombing. Before long we've found a useful solid table, a 200-litre plastic barrel and some long straight boards. Anne wants to collect all the smoky green glass balls that lie along the beach. 'What are you going to do with them?' I ask. I have already had this impulse and logically decided only to gather a certain reasonable amount. 'We already have more than twenty around the house.'

'They're so pretty,' Anne replies. 'We can't just leave them all here on the beach.'

'And we can't take them all, either,' I say. 'There are too many.'

After our picnic of grilled jack and a look at the tank and the old marae temple ruins, we're ready to return. First we place the table upside-down across *Mini-Mini*, then load on the plastic barrel and long boards. Anne fits in as many of the pretty glass fishing buoys as possible.

We are too heavy and have difficulty sailing. After one hour underway we decide to make a stop at one of the islets where there are hundreds of migrating sooty terns circling around and around. As we go ashore, hundreds of the nesting birds rise from the ground. Angry at our intrusion, they dive at us again and again until their shrieking and screaming dominate everything. The sounds penetrate deep into our heads to dull our senses. Kiki is terrified and stays close and low with her tail between her legs. The children are also afraid. We hold hands in solidarity to combat our Hitchcockian aggressors.

'Look for eggs,' I shout above the noise. After a quick search it becomes evident that the terns have not yet begun to lay. 'We'll have to come back in one or two weeks,' I say.

'Then we'll have a big omelette!' Anaïs suggests enthusiastically.

'What about their babies?' Alexandre asks.

'If we take away their first egg, they'll lay again like the hens,' I say.

'Is that true?' Anne asks.

'I don't know, but someone once told me that, and it eases my conscience to believe it's true.'

'As I see it, you would believe anything to ease your precious conscience!' she states.

'I'm not alone,' I respond.

Ten days pass before I decide to head back up the lagoon. I'm on my own this time. I rest low in *Mini-Mini* with only my head showing over the sides of the dinghy. The wind being light, the dinghy sails along sweetly to the music of the wind and rhythmic tap-tapping of water rolling along its sides. For a long time nothing exists except my movement through the water. The sun is warm and comfortable. I float through time on my tiny spaceship, free as a spaceman in a universe that has no beginning and no end.

The screeching of birds enters my dulled senses as I arrive ashore on the islet. Now there are hundreds of eggs. They should all be fresh. Just the same I methodically plunge each egg in a container of seawater to check that it doesn't float and is therefore fresh. I take enough for a few days' omelettes, then return to my dream world. I drift into my floating abstraction again as I glide back down the lagoon, my mind empty in the present, yet full and aware of my part in the whole. Questions and answers, good and bad, right and wrong are of no significance – all is one. I am at one with all.

Some years previously we established the civilised routine of three meals each day at regular times to give a little structure to an otherwise unstructured cruising life.

This broke the day up conveniently and gave us a system to work around during the day. It never became an obsession, but it did develop into a solid habit that was rarely broken. We continued this routine on Caroline. Around the meal table we never say 'grace' in the Christian manner, but we are always respectful and often vocal in our thanks for all the food provided for us by the grace of our natural surroundings. It is very special to live close to the land where one develops the comfortable feeling that nature is on one's side, providing gifts and reassurance every day.

Most people don't appear to give much thought to the dramatic fact that our wonderful spinning planet is an enormous ball of fire that has been blazing with incredible intensity for millions of years. Maybe one day someone will explain to me how it just keeps going without fuel or oxygen. Here on the cooled surface of Caroline I have my own fire problems. For the three ritual meals of the day I require three fires. As the months have passed, I've had to go farther and farther into the forest to collect my firewood. What I'm slow to realise is that instead of regular wood I could use up the constant and annoying pile of half coconut husks that gathers around the house. All I have to do is split them one more time and store them dry under the benches of the cookhouse. Since coconut husks burn faster than wood, I need to spend a little more time keeping the fire constantly stoked up. But time is still plentiful here, and it's less trouble to attend to the fire this way than to search far for daily firewood.

'The perfect system,' I explain with satisfaction to Anne. 'You collect the coconuts and split them for the hens. I pick them up and burn them. The hens are fed, the yard remains clear and we always have fuel. Now, that's what I call a really sensible and environmentally sympathetic system.'

'You could use the ashes for the garden too,' she adds.

The Polynesians blend in with the processes of nature around them when they bleed the rich sap that flows up through the coconut trees. This twice-daily routine takes on the form of a ritual. Each time they climb up their tree, they chant a special song. Then they transfer the sap that has collected since their previous visit into a bottle, and make a fresh fine cut into the source, an unopened pod of coconut buds, and replace the collecting jar. They repeat this whole operation every twelve hours and use the collected sap, which is rich in sugar and contains natural yeast, to produce a strong coconut beer that is known as 'toddy'. Boiled down, this sap concentrates into a golden syrup, and further heating turns it into a solid toffee.

I'm not interested in becoming involved in the tree-climbing, sap-bleeding operation. I have another idea, however: to boil down the water inside the plentiful green coconuts. I have to assume there is some connection between the trees' sweet sap and the sweet coconut water. It takes a good number of coconuts and time, but it works. I show Anne my full jar of concentrated honey-coloured sweet syrup.

'Genius,' she says with a big smile.

'Elementary,' I correct modestly. 'Anyway, I don't particularly want to be a genius. It's geniuses who have upset our world and led us to where we are today: Bell with his telephone, Ford with his cars, Einstein with his bomb. If it had been left to normal people like me, we would still be living out normal lives.'

'Like how?' she asks, looking a little bored with my philosophising.

'Like the old Polynesians, families taking from their surroundings only what they need for the day, refusing any organised progress. They don't encourage geniuses. In fact, anyone manifesting extra brains in Polynesian society is socially isolated so as to protect the unity of the rest of the community – even their chiefs. When they become too big for their boots, they change them.'

'Now there's a smart idea,' she says, looking sideways at me. 'Anyway, brains have made some progress,' she continues. 'What about education?'

'Knowledge is infinite,' I respond quickly as I sense another chance to air the thoughts that constantly turn inside my head. 'We can never hope to know everything about everything, even if we had the ability to sense everything. What we do is use our limited senses and information to develop certain popular themes. All the intellectual meddling and messing that we do has little or no impact on the real forces that control our destiny. We carry out our actions and interactions within our fixed characters, and then we justify them with intellectual arguments and alibis. What finally happens is that we find our real comfort in an imagined world of total fantasy. Which in fact ignores the few facts that we have uncovered.'

'Well, well, aren't we negative?' she replies.

'It's not negative,' I say, warming to my new theme. 'If I can prove to myself that every last person is lost in the wilderness that is himself and his immediate environment, then I don't have to listen to all the serious preachers – and that's a great load off my mind.'

'Sign me up for the anti-preacher club,' she laughs.

'We exist in a live-and-let-live system; we defend our space and try to survive in the jungle, just as the plants do.'

'I don't happen to see myself as a plant!' she says indignantly.

'Plants are and remain basic,' I respond. 'We, underneath it all, are also basic. The difference is we left the jungle to try to escape the basics. The trouble is we walked out with our basic genes, which, like those of the plants, fundamentally still consider personal survival a pretty important priority. We pretend to ourselves, but we simply continue the survival fight in our new jungle. And here, despite periods of relatively organised calm, the real forces keep re-emerging. They sometimes come with explosive power and cause terrible bloodshed. That's the system, even if you don't want to see it. It's active, aggressive, opportunistic and won't go away. Better to join it.'

'I've joined the human race,' she muses, deep in thought.

'It's not all bad news,' I smile. 'There are lots of powerful attractions and erotic little affairs that bring all the little yins and yangs sliding together to indulge in wonderful passionate love-ins.'

'With you, nothing is sacred,' she states in disgust.

'If we feel the necessity to get down on our humble knees and worship something sacred and all-powerful, the source of our individual lives, the source of everything, it should be this ultimate original force. This force which made us, and despite our meddling attempts to oppose its domination, keeps us alive.'

'Very interesting,' she smiles, 'so what do we do?'

'We do as we've always done – remain its slaves. There's no escape. We can build towers, palaces and pyramids, create grand religions, start wars, join a circus or find a mate and run away to an uninhabited island – all interesting projects to while away an hour or two. But in the larger scheme of things our actions change nothing.'

'You're a real pessimist with no real conclusions,' she says.

'No I'm not,' I insist. 'Pessimists stay at home, cry into their beer and keep up their insurance payments. My conclusion is to try to accept these realities of life and find a comfortable place to play out my time.'

Anne, who has had enough of my philosophising, wanders off to prepare for her fishing trip. I continue thinking alone. Our age has been a disaster. For reasons of religion, colour, class, or because of the insane ideals, whims or greed of an individual, millions and millions of people have been killed this century. And mostly for lost causes. We are surely fumbling. Maybe it's time to sit quietly and look hard at the basics and fundamentals of our natures. That's why I'm here. Our natures won't change, no matter how much civilising or training we inflict on them; that seems certain. With survival our main priority, we have to remain opportunistic and expansionist as individuals.

In the real jungle, this potential aggression is limited by the difficult surroundings and continual interference of similarly motivated, tough neighbours. This results in a certain balance and stability based on aggression. In a society based on friendly brotherhood and controlled behaviour it's quite different. Opportunists, provided they stay more or less within the law, are free to expand their wealth and power and impose their views, however distorted, on the lives of ordinary people. I find this frightening and very disturbing. When I was a contributing part of modern progressive society, I made a sincere effort to be a good citizen, but I always had the feeling that the system as a whole wasn't backing me up. I was too serious. What I didn't realise then was that organised society is simply a man-made ideal, a disciplined game against nature with lots of controlling do's and taboos.

Polynesians, like us, face a daily struggle. They differ inasmuch as they, for whatever reason, are less serious and intense. This allows them to hold on to their developed sense of fun and pleasure. They take their time and remain true to their long-established culture. They show a rare sincerity when participating in their traditional dancing, sports and rhythmic music. Compared to our modern consumer culture, the Polynesians, who are experts on working together as a close community, could teach us many things about the simple enjoyment of being alive. With that final thought, I wander on to join in the fun and practical tasks of survival on Caroline.

Later in the morning Anne returns in good spirits with her bucket full of big red snappers and large groupers. 'You have to come and see my new fishing place,' she exults. 'It's right out on the reef just behind Ana-Ana.'

Next day we follow her out to a raised area of coral that runs alongside a large deep crack connecting to the open sea. Alexandre passes the bait while Anaïs holds my hand and the bucket. Kiki can't decide whether to stay on our little refuge of high coral or wander to the safety of the dry reef. For the moment, she stays.

Anne quickly catches a grouper, then a large red snapper. We share the pleasure of her success, too preoccupied at first to notice the slow build-up of the swells. A little alarmed, I begin to move in toward the dry reef with the children. Suddenly a bigger swell runs in and swirls around our legs. Anne has seen it coming and moves to join us on the highest spot of our diminishing refuge.

The next swell rushes up to our knees with great force and sweeps Anaïs off her feet. Alexandre hangs on to my waist while I brace myself against the current to stay upright. Kiki is swept away toward the dry reef and immediately starts yelping. 'The dog is caught on your hook!' I shout to Anne as I start for the shore. 'Let your line go, and let's get out of here.'

The backwash has other ideas and tries to pull us down into the open crack and out to the open sea. The next swell hits our backs and both children are swept off their feet. Alexandre hangs on fiercely with his arms around my neck. I lock my hand on Anaïs's and struggle desperately to remain upright as I stumble on towards the shore. One of my shoes slips off. I continue on through the outgoing foam until we arrive safely on the dry reef. The dog, after being freed from the hook and line, is waiting for us.

We count our losses. 'I've saved the fish, but lost my shoe,' I say breathlessly as I hand the bucket to Anne.

'*Merde!*' she says. 'The roll of nylon and the hooks are not in the bucket. It was the last roll of fishing nylon.'

The swells subside a little. I limp back around the coral islet to look for the nylon and my precious plastic shoe. The box of hooks comes floating in on a wave. The nylon and my shoe have been sucked down the hole.

'I was really scared,' Alexandre says quietly as he comes to terms with his fear. He is still very tense.

'Me too,' I say – for I know well the danger of the sudden inrush of tons of water. If you happen to be knocked down, the breaking waves and sharp coral can easily cause lacerations, broken bones and worse. We had reason to be scared.

In general, we watch the children almost too much. We know where they are every minute of each day. They are warned to play only in the lower branches of the trees, and not to swim alone in the lagoon.

Already we have found on South Islet one tombstone marked: 'William Brothers born March 15th 1865. Died at sea April 19th 1866'. A one-year-old child. That stone haunts us. Anne has cleared out the underbrush around it and periodically places flowers near it.

'I have a big boat now,' Alexandre informs us not long after the fishing incident. 'It's there behind Ana-Ana, and it's ready to go.' I know they use a big rock out on the reef as a radio station. The boat is a new creation of their imaginations. 'I talk to it every day,' he continues. 'If you need rice, flour, new shoes or nylon, it's okay. My big boat will get it.' I marvel at the processes of the human mind. Faced with anxiety and an insoluble practical situation, he has found his own abstract solution in fantasy. He ignores any direct questions about his phantom boat. 'Don't worry,' he repeats sincerely to all our questions. 'It's there if you need it.'

Fortunately, we don't have to test the mythical big boat saviour. In a fresh search aboard *Fleur d'Ecosse* I find another reel of light nylon. I also unpack my last pair of plastic reef shoes.

So far we've eaten fourteen pumpkins, which Anne claims as her success. Every morning as she does her garden inspection she picks a male flower and gently vibrates the stamen deep inside each female. A few days after her marriage ceremonies – which are absolutely essential, she claims, as we have no bees here – she's proud to show us each new developing baby. Her other success is the multiplication of the hens. Now they number twenty-five and give us a regular supply of eggs. We take out an occasional extra cock for Sunday's roast. To help Omer with his growing harem, we've reserved one cock for stud duties. We've named him Papa-Ya.

When July comes, all our supplies, including those brought by George, are finished. We plan to sail first back to Ahe for the rest of our belongings, then continue on to Tahiti for a shopping trip and haul-out for the boat.

We also have an arrangement to meet Anne's parents, who are visiting Polynesia at the beginning of September. We're a little uneasy at the prospect of this encounter since they have been dubious, at best, about our adventure from the start.

13

A Brief Return to Civilisation

I've gone aboard *Fleur d'Ecosse* fairly regularly during our stay to run the motor and check the mooring lines. With all the other priorities, I have done little maintenance. I take one week off to overhaul the motor, windvane autopilot, pressure stove, sails and rigging. Finally, I go over the side among the sharks to clean off ten months' growth of barnacles from the bottom. Fortunately, the sharks appear to accept my familiar presence. They circle around close by to check out my activities, but they don't attack.

Alexandre and Anaïs are not troubled at all by the idea of leaving the island – they're simply excited to be going on another adventure. Anne also, with her sense of correct procedure, shows little distress during the preparations. But for me it's difficult to think about leaving, even for a short time. I feel quiet and at peace here. Facing the turmoil of the outside world is going to be hard.

We move the radio aboard. Items like the solar panels and tools we hide in the jungle. *Mini-Mini* is dragged into the bushes, turned over and covered with coconut leaves. Finally the hens, who usually spend half their time locked in their run to discourage them from laying eggs in the jungle, are turned loose. I leave them a system that will provide regular water.

We leave a note fixed to the kitchen shelf:

We have to leave temporarily for provisions. We'll be back soon. Please don't take our belongings. Help yourself to eggs or fruit. Please leave your name and the name of your vessel.

Ron, Anne, Alexandre and Anaïs Falconer

As we leave our little settlement, I am frozen for a moment by a wave of panic that courses through my body. Whether this is my kingdom or my prison I don't know, but this is where I can be myself. Only the sure thought that we will be back allows me finally to walk away.

After all our freedom ashore the boat seems small. Kiki prowls unhappily on deck while Dou-Dou sulks into a listless sleep. The parakeets hang again from their familiar hook, making their familiar mess on my chart table. Settled aboard, the children dig out their toys. Once more the floor and main passageway through the boat become a dangerous maze of plastic building materials.

The wind is too strong to exit the pass. We profit from the four days of enforced rest to become familiar again with the boat and pick up our old routines. When we finally take to the open sea, the wind is light and favourable from the northeast. We can follow a direct course to Ahe.

Each time we come back to Ahe, it feels like a home-coming. As soon as we arrive, we're warmly greeted by Mama Fana and Papa Toa. Straightaway we are invited to share a meal with all our friends. On the island they have an agreeable and established custom that when villagers return after a long period of absence, they become the complete centre of attention for an afternoon or an evening. Now it's our turn.

They are impressed by the size of the fish we caught, the number of coconut crabs, the thousands of birds, the lobsters and the turtles. We discuss the marae. One old man remembers the names of some Polynesians who worked on the copra plantation there in the early 1900s.

As we wander through the village back to the boat, the children are excited. When they see flowers in a garden, they simply walk in and help themselves. 'You can't do that,' I say, a little taken aback.

'Why not?' they ask together.

'Because the flowers belong to somebody. They're private,' I reply.

'They aren't private on Caroline,' Alexandre says.

'Caroline's different. Here people have separate gardens that belong to them.'

'Oh!' he says in some surprise. 'Does Caroline belong to us, then?'

'No, we just live there with the permission of Captain Darr,' I say.

'Does it belong to Captain Darr, then?' he persists.

'Well, no. Captain Darr only had permission from the government of Great Britain.'

'So it belongs to Great Britain,' he states.

'Well, no. Ten years ago the government of Great Britain gave it to the government of Kiribati, which is a new Pacific Ocean nation formed from the old Gilbert Islands. Now Captain Omer Darr has permission from this Republic of Kiribati, and we have permission from Captain Omer Darr.'

'Oh.' He's somewhat confused, but at least he has understood a little about land ownership – and that gardens and islands, even deserted ones, all belong to somebody.

It's good to be back on Ahe even though I have the feeling that this represents an era in our life that has passed. We are an accepted part of this large village family of around one hundred people. Nevertheless, here we always remain 'the guests'. On Caroline we are free to live as we wish with our own particular mix of Polynesian and European traditions. On Caroline we have the unique luxury of freedom, time and space, to work out our own priorities and value system.

We do one last clean-up of our old A-frame hut where Alexandre and Anaïs were babies. When it's time to travel on, it seems too soon. Again we take part in the farewell ceremonies. Light-hearted banter disguises our sadness when we eventually take our leave.

Papeete town is something else. We stand on the quay and simply stare amazed at the nose-to-tail speeding cars, trucks and motorcycles. So much colour and noise, and so many smells. So many people. We find ourselves staring into the faces of passing individuals as if we had arrived from another planet. We look intently at their expressions, the shape of their noses, lips and eyes. Are town-dwellers really so different from us?

'Look at that dress,' Anne says in total amazement.

'And look at that haircut,' I add.

Maybe it's only style; I'm not sure. I do know that after twenty-four hours our fascination dies. Our open-mouthed tourist look is replaced by a more knowing, serious expression. We, like the locals, have business to attend to.

On the boat slip I meet Joseph, who is also anti-fouling his yacht. In the evening we have a chance to talk. He tells me he lives in Tahiti and has sailed around the islands for many years. He is interested in our experiences on Caroline. When I talk about the pollinating of the pumpkins and tomatoes by hand, he says thoughtfully, 'I wonder how bees would survive on a coral island?'

'We don't have many flowers as such,' I explain. 'Only the blossoms on the trees, or perhaps the coconut tree has pollen.'

Joseph explains that he's a beekeeper with hives on Tahiti and Moorea. 'I'd be really interested to see how bees would do on a coral island,' he repeats.

'Well, some honey would be useful,' I say, 'but I know nothing at all about bee-keeping.'

'If you like,' he says, 'I'll take you up to my house and show you the basics. I have a hive kit that's not too expensive, and perhaps I can find you an old smoker. You don't need many things to start. Before you leave, I can give you a small swarm complete with a queen.'

'You're going to take a hive of bees on the boat?' Anne asks me in open dismay.

'I imagine they'll be sealed in,' I reply, hoping that's true.

Joseph arrives the day after to take us up to his house. It's isolated and high in the mountains above Papeete. He has a swimming pool and a spectacular view out over the sea. After introducing us to his wife, he takes us around to the back of the house.

'Look, there's the queen.' Joseph points to a cluster of bees on a honeycomb he has just removed from a hive. 'Watch how the workers protect her.' I imagine I see the queen, and what he has done to extract the comb doesn't seem too difficult. All the same, I'm not so sure how brave I would be if I had to do it on my own.

'I'm afraid,' Anne says.

'You're not alone,' I sympathise.

Nevertheless, after more discussions over tea and cakes, it's generally agreed that we will have a try at beekeeping on Caroline.

For our shopping this time, Anne calculates her list in reverse of her rationing. She multiplies one day's normal supplies by seven, then by fifty-two. The final amounts are impressive.

'One ton is the maximum weight the boat will take,' I warn her.

'Where are we going to store one ton of food?' she asks.

'I don't know,' I reply. 'On the floor, on the bed – we'll sleep on top of it if we have to.'

After spending a day checking out the big stores, she finds Win Chong will provide full boxes of supplies at ten per cent discount and Cash and Carry can supply most of the other things. 'Plus, they both deliver free,' she adds with satisfaction.

The boxes begin to arrive: canned milk, tinned butter, oil, brown rice, flour, wheat, sugar and beans. As fast as I can transfer them aboard, new supplies arrive. 'Do we really need all this stuff?' I ask as I desperately try to pack everything to create maximum space.

'Yes, we do!' is all she replies. Obviously, one food crisis was enough.

The boxes build higher and higher. *Fleur d'Ecosse* settles lower and lower in the water. Over the years as more and more cruising gear has collected aboard, I've already raised the painted waterline of the boat twice. Once more the waterline disappears beneath the surface, as does the exhaust exit of the motor, which now bubbles out its diesel fumes underwater.

Our special purchase this year is a sack of wheat grain. Normal white flour goes flat and stale after only three months, while wheat grains stay alive and fresh for years. When ground, wheat grains provide a rich, fibrous, complete flour. All I need is a wheat grinder. The Chinese storekeepers look at me as if I'm searching for a vintage car.

'A wheat grinder? Ahh haa!' they repeat. 'What does it look like?'

I find a shopkeeper who used to stock them. 'No more,' he says. 'No demand.'

In desperation I begin a yacht-to-yacht search with the standard greeting: 'Excuse me, but I don't suppose you have a wheat grinder to sell?'

One yacht owner hesitates, then says, 'Well, yes, we do have a small wheat grinder, why?'

I explain my story, and they bring out the grinder. It's not small, it's tiny – something you attach to the breakfast table to grind a few grains to add to your muesli.

'I have a whole sackful of wheat,' I say in distress. But I've found nothing else, so I take the grinder.

'It's not just tiny, it's ridiculous!' Anne states when she sees it.

Before leaving Papeete, we're invited to a local restaurant for what they humorously call a 'bored' meeting of the coffee klatch net. There we meet Les and Little Earl for the first time. Les has become an understanding and helpful friend in our isolation. It's an odd feeling to meet this physical stranger, whom I recognise by his deep voice. He's tall and thin, to the point of being gaunt. He's also older than I had imagined.

The regular meeting of the coffee klatch net at eight o'clock every Monday, Wednesday and Friday has been our main source of news and information. Members of this small, dedicated group of amateur radio operators are mostly based around Polynesia. However, we are regularly joined by operators on Christmas Island, Hawaii and the Cook Islands. The subject of conversation varies from local weather and sailing conditions, day-to-day maintenance problems and anything else of interest such as the price of beer. It's a bit like your local pub: a place where people drop in fairly regularly to chat and gossip with one another. In our isolation it's an added bonus to be able to share our adventures with regular listeners.

It's time to leave the hustle and bustle of Papeete. We quickly arrange our clearance papers and abandon the big city to sail the short distance to Moorea. We anchor just in front of the Kia-Ora Hotel, where Anne's parents are staying. We had met them together as a family only once before, in Polynesia, when they came to Rangiroa to see Alexandre and Anaïs for the first time. So we spend some time getting reacquainted.

We take turns standing under the plentiful hot water that gushes freely from the shower facilities in their elegant beach bungalow. Unfortunately these pleasures are counter-balanced by tensions. Anne's parents, understandably I suppose, are fearful for the safety of their grandchildren. They are against the idea of our returning to Caroline. I sense that my presence will not help ease the conflict, so, using the excuse that I need to spend some time with Captain Omer Darr, I leave Anne and the children to enjoy a little hotel comfort and smooth out relationships with her parents. I sail alone the short distance to the dark tranquil waters of Opunohu Bay.

I have the whole bay to myself. For the first time since we arrived, I can breathe easily. I spend two days in peaceful bliss before summoning up the necessary energy for a visit to Omer Darr. When he invites me into his small sitting room for a glass of wine, I have to make my way over and through at least twenty-five cats of various ages that lie sprawled out all over his veranda.

'You have a cat, if I remember correctly?' he says as an offhand greeting.

'Yes,' I say, 'a female.'

'You have to be very careful,' he goes on. 'They breed very fast, you know. On Christmas Island they developed into a real problem. They killed so many of the young seabirds they upset the whole balance of nature. On Caroline your cat could be a problem.'

I glance out at the veranda and think back to all the times that poor Dou-Dou has scoured the jungle, meowing pitifully as she desperately searched for a playmate. I nod sagely to indicate agreement, though it's clear that out-of-control cat breeding is more his problem than mine.

'What about your lease?' I ask. 'Do you have any possibility of renewing it?'

He sips his drink and looks around a little. 'I'm still trying, it's a problem of communicating,' he says quietly. 'The Kiribati people won't reply to my letters. They aren't at all like the old British government officials, who've always replied quickly and efficiently to all my correspondence.'

I feel a shiver of apprehension. This is a threat to our status on Caroline. But Omer moves on to another problem he wants to talk about. Harriet, his wife, has had to go to Hawaii, and tomorrow he leaves to join her. His housekeeper will look after the house, but he needs someone to exercise his guard dogs twice a day for the next two weeks.

The guard dogs are four large Alsatians that are firmly chained to each corner of the house. The first three he introduces me to are reasonable to handle. The fourth one lunges to the limit of its chain and grabs my knee. I jump back fast but have two clear and painful teeth marks on my kneecap. 'How am I going to walk this creature on my own?' I question.

'He'll be all right when he gets to know you,' Omer tries to reassure me.

That night I eat at the hotel with my parents-in-law. Anne's father finds my problem amusing. 'That's the price of your rent,' he smiles.

The subject of Caroline is not brought up, and I can't tell from Anne's expression whether he has changed his position about our new home. He introduces his own problem: what to do with his large and heavily taxed income. Never having had the luxury of this kind of dilemma, I have little to contribute.

At his invitation I order a large beefsteak. I save half of it to take back to the boat.

In the morning, after walking the three calm dogs, I brave the monster. He stands on his hind legs, his chain taut. He stares at me, frothing at the mouth and growling. I sit down just out of his reach and unwrap the beefsteak. He watches me carefully until eventually I throw him a tiny morsel. The change is instantaneous. He sits down, adopts a soft goofy look and with a cocked head watches my every move. Slowly I dole out more tiny pieces of top-quality bribery steak.

He's bought. He sits there drooling and dribbling in adoration of his new patron. On the walk I carry a stick just in case there is any sign of infidelity, but he behaves well. From then on, each time I arrive he wags his tail, sits down, and then waits patiently in anticipation of a possible handout from his new friend.

I profit from Omer's large property to collect banana shoots and small breadfruit, mango and tamarind trees. As I transplant my collection into plastic bags, I envy Omer all his rich black soil. I continue by taking cuttings from the Tiare of Tahiti and the frangipani and hibiscus bushes.

Anne arrives at the boat depressed. Her parents have in fact been difficult. They are completely against taking the children back to Caroline, since they think this kind of upbringing will affect their characters and that they will turn out to be antisocial. I say as little as possible, knowing that I can depend on the rebel in Anne to take the opposite line against any outside pressures to organise her life. I don't think the children will become antisocial. They're secure with two caring parents to attend to and protect them, twenty-four hours a day. We share fun and problems together. They live real lives in a real world. Eventually they'll have to live with other people and face the challenges thrown up by their own particular characters, but that's something everyone has to do. I don't think they'll be handicapped in any way by their adventuring background.

In a previous discussion Anne did bring up one of her personal worries about our situation. If something terrible did happen to the children and they could have been saved by medical assistance, how would she be able to live with her own conscience?

There are always risks in life, and as far as I'm concerned, keeping on your toes helps you stay alive. All things considered, the children's physical health is safer on Caroline than it would be in a city full of cars, pollution and crime. I remember that when I left Scotland for the first time I was worried, as was my family, about my high-risk adventure. Having made it halfway round the world with nothing more serious than minor cuts and bruises, I received a letter from my mother, who told me that a cousin in America had been seriously injured in a car accident. She had fallen asleep while driving on the freeway.

We are all prepared to leave. Down below, the boxes completely fill the passageway and cover the beds. We arrange the mattresses over the top to form a sleeping area high above the floor level. The front toilet compartment is crammed with plants and is now unusable.

Joseph faithfully arrives at the last moment with a small hive full of humming bees. He has also brought along a kit to construct a proper hive, as well as a smoker and a book on beekeeping. Dou-Dou adds to our nervous state by immediately peeling off a piece of the mesh that covers a ventilation hole. A few bees escape into the boat before I can reseal the mesh and reinforce it with sticky tape. I explain very clearly to Dou-Dou that if she as much as touches the hive again, she will be hung, drawn, quartered and tossed overboard. Then I cattily add, 'Omer is against you coming back anyway.'

We cast off to begin our trip back to Caroline Atoll. Moorea slowly sinks down into the sea, finally to fade into the darkness of the night. The wind is moderate and warm, the sky clear with bright stars. Everyone is soon asleep. I pull out a little secret package that I bought for myself while shopping in Papeete: a chromatic harmonica. Once or twice I've tried to master this relatively simple instrument, but with little success. I quietly blow, blow, suck, blow, over and over again as we slowly plough our way north, until my first little tune begins to appear:

Oh, when the Saints,
Oh, when the Saints,
Oh, when the Saints
Come marching in . . .

And then I add my own final line:

We're sailing home,
We're sailing home,
We're sailing home,
Back to Caroline!

14

A Disquieting Meeting with the Future

With a regular easy rhythm, the ocean miles slide by as we again sail due north toward the equator. Thoughts of our home are strong in our minds as we anticipate a return to the peace and contentment we found on Caroline. Any apprehension that established itself on Moorea has been absorbed by the healing action of the open ocean and thoughts of calm isolation on our special island.

Just before sunset we sight the highest treetops of Caroline's islets. Because of the curvature of the earth and the fairly constant height of coconut trees, I know by experience that we still have about ten miles to go before we actually reach the island. Since we will arrive too late to enter the pass, we head directly for Nake Islet to spend the night hove-to in the shelter of the lee side.

The orange sunset darkens with the last light of the day, and the full round moon, rising slowly, appears over the eastern horizon. Then I see a light!

'It's on Nake Islet,' I state confidently, although I'm not sure.

'It's moving,' Anne says, and I wonder if the extraterrestrials have been visiting during our absence.

'Maybe it's a UFO,' I suggest. 'They've spotted us and are now clearing out.'

'More likely a boat behind the island,' says the practical Anne.

'Maybe,' I reason, 'but if it's a boat that's fishing, they're breaking the law. If we surprise them, there's a chance they could run us down rather than risk being reported and having their boat and equipment confiscated.'

'They wouldn't dare,' Anne says with indignation.

In this area there are Russian, Korean and Japanese fishing boats. They fish with long lines and stay offshore for months at a time. I was told that released convicts often man them. Who knows what could happen? I switch on the VHF. If I can find out who or what is around the island, we still have a chance to slide off into the darkness. 'Hello, hello,' I call into the night. 'This is a sailing boat off Caroline Atoll; do you have any copy?'

A minute of total silence passes before I repeat the call. Then we sit and wait again.

'Tigress, Tigress,' the radio bursts into our silence. 'We have a poor copy on you. We will see you in the morning.' It's a male voice with a very strong foreign accent. I look at Anne, but she indicates with a shrug that she understands no more than I do.

'Hello, hello, this is a sailing boat. Do you have a copy?' I repeat. A longer pause follows before the same voice says, 'Yes, we have a copy. Please wait.' The minutes tick by before a female voice, also foreign, garbles a long sentence of which I understand only the one word: 'Tigress.'

I try again. 'This is a sailing boat, a yacht, off Caroline Atoll. Do you copy?'

'Oh, a yacht, yes, yes, a yacht.' There is understanding in the tone of her reply but also a questioning. Then the radio remains silent.

'Hello, hello.' I try to sound light and social and speak slowly. 'We can see your lights. What are you doing here?'

'Please repeat,' the voice says. 'Your signal is breaking up.'

'What are you doing here?' I repeat. I'm not sure if they really have a problem with my signal or if they're playing for time while they line us up on their armament system for immediate extermination.

'We're working,' comes back the short reply.

Working what, I wonder? 'Are you fishing?' I finally ask.

'We're working,' comes the same short reply. There appears little more to be gained from continuing this difficult conversation. I wish the female operator a polite goodnight.

'So, what do you think?' I ask Anne.

'It all seems a bit strange. They could be a fishing boat, but who or what is Tigress?'

'Could be two boats,' I suggest.

'Or a group of predator space visitors,' Anne smiles.

There's little we can do, but for our peace of mind I change radios and find Les on the evening maritime net.

'We're not sure what to make of it, Les,' I finish, 'but if we're not here in the morning, you'll know we are either at the bottom of the ocean or on our way to another planet.'

As we approach Nake Islet, the light slowly moves away to the west and fades over the horizon to disappear along with the setting stars.

'That's that,' I say with some relief. 'Whatever it was, we've succeeded in scaring them away.'

'A gold star for the guardian!' Anne remarks.

Sheltered behind the island, our watches pass peacefully. The full moon marks the passing hours as it traces its slow path from east to west. The moon sets just before the darkness softens into daylight, letting the green islets reappear in front of our eyes. The morning sky changes from watery blue to rich red and another new day is born.

Our cockpit breakfast comes to an abrupt halt when I spot three men on the beach at South Islet. They stand still, watching us, as amazed to see us as we are to see them. They have an inflatable Zodiac dinghy close alongside them. 'That's Tigress,' Anne guesses. 'Try to call them.'

'Well, good morning,' a clear American voice replies to my VHF message. We slip quickly into an easy and comfortable conversation. He tells us his name is Greg, he has two colleagues with him and they are part of a Russian-American survey team doing a scientific study of Caroline.

'Are you Tigress?' I ask.

'No,' he replies, 'Tigress is another team of biologists who have a camp on Nake Islet. Our call sign here is Zodiac.'

'And your ship?' I have to believe him, but the whole situation still seems incredible.

'The ship is Russian,' he replies, 'and it'll arrive back soon. They have their own laboratory and survey equipment aboard. We're only a small attached American team.'

His story seems reasonable, but the fears of the night before remain fresh in my mind. I now consider the possibility that they could also all be Russian and that they have chosen isolated Caroline to set up a communications spy station.

Omitting the fact that we live here, I say only that we are going to take a look at the pass on the east side. Going around South Islet, I'm desperate to be ashore, take possession of our house and establish our place in front of all these strangers. Unfortunately, the wind is strong and the pass is a mass of white water. Although I have plenty of reasons to take a risk, it's too dangerous. We return once more to wait out the weather and anchor close into the reef of South Islet.

'There's a big ship coming,' Alexandre announces as we finally let out our second anchor. The big ship, comparable to a passenger liner, draws to a stop just behind us, making no attempt to anchor. I read *AKADEMIK KOROLEV* boldly painted on a huge board. Scientific-looking round shiny domes and slowly turning radar antennas adorn the top deck to dominate the skyline. We stare up in awe at this huge apparition so close behind us. They lower a red lifeboat into the sea. I'm nervous and not at all sure that they won't board us with guns. When they ignore us completely and proceed to unload personnel and equipment onto the reef, I'm a little disappointed that they didn't even bother to say good morning.

I count twelve people, both male and female, as they move with difficulty, despite the relatively calm swells, from the surging lifeboat onto the dry reef. Each person carries a piece of equipment. They head in across the reef in a long straight line like shipwrecked pirates transporting ashore all the booty they have saved from their abandoned vessel. Their numbers intimidate the local sharks. Not one attempts a confrontation with the newest invaders.

'We're still here,' I confirm to Les on the morning net. Then I fill him in on the revelations and activities of our surprise visitors.

'Too bad, Ron. You think you've escaped, but the busy world is never far behind,' Les says, commiserating with us.

It's too bad about everything. We feel like people who are stuck in their car on the street outside their house while they watch strangers swarm all over their garden. I also have a hive of bees that are desperate for their freedom.

I take the dinghy ashore. First I encounter the Americans, who have installed themselves at our Puti-Puti base camp. They are busy 'working'. Greg takes time off to explain that they are looking for the presence of particular small floating plastic beads. These beads, he says, are the eventual breakdown of all the plastic debris that finds its way into the oceans. The problem is that these beads are now present throughout the world in every ocean and are being eaten by fish. This, he informs me, could eventually cause widespread health problems. Their 'work' is to drag a fine net across Caroline's lagoon, then do a bead count.

'The biologists are a married couple,' Greg goes on to explain, 'Cam and Kay Kepler. They're doing a systematic survey of all the separate islets for a bird and fauna analysis. They also have with them a representative from the Republic of Kiribati, Katino, who normally lives on Christmas Island.'

'I'm acting as guardian for a Captain Omer Darr, who has the private lease on this atoll,' I tell them eventually. 'I know nothing about this survey. My house is on an islet just north of here.'

'I saw your house yesterday,' one of Greg's colleagues says, 'and your hens.'

With the news of the hens I'm anxious to pay a quick visit to the house. On my way back along the beach, I stop in on the Russian camp. As I enter the bushes, a young man approaches me. He replies very politely in good English to my greeting of good morning. I explain once more who we are, and about our house and the children.

As I speak, he translates each piece of information for the onlooking attentive group. They nod their heads in understanding. I can see by their expressions that they are having some difficulties accepting the truth of our story.

He says that their 'work' is to take water samples from the lagoon. Their chief professor stands not far away. He has a short round body, large head, and goatee beard. With his town suit and a big cigar, he looks more appropriately outfitted for a Walt Disney movie set than for a tropical island workstation. From their supplies, they present me with a huge traditional Russian black loaf and some oranges. 'For the children,' the translator explains.

On the beach I hesitate for a moment as I sense that one of the two girls who were busy filling test tubes has followed me out.

'I like Scottish boys,' she says in a low sultry voice. She's young and pretty. I immediately wonder if she is simply being polite or has some other motivation in mind.

'Especially your national poet Robert Burns,' she adds.

In reply, I recite the first few lines of 'Ode to a Mouse' from my long-lost school days.

She laughs and moves in closer. Now I'm sure she has some other motive in mind and wonder if, in fact, she wants to defect.

I imagine Anne having to share the island with an attractive Russian female defector and hesitate between the temptations of polygamy and my anxiety to check out the hens. Finally, I give her a polite kiss on each of her white cheeks, warn her about the tropical sun and explain that I really must go and check on my hens.

Back on board, after checking the house, I'm well received with my black bread, oranges and news. I say nothing about the 'Robert Burns' recital, telling them instead that the house is okay and that I found three of the hens.

Next morning the bees take priority. They seem to be dying and have to be moved ashore as soon as possible. Since the base and roof of the new hive are ready, all I have to do is construct the square box sections and assemble the numerous combs for the honey.

Two eager children compete to 'pass the glue' or give me 'another nail please'. The work proceeds as a new game. We're so absorbed that we hardly notice the arrival of the morning big ship and the landing of the work team on the reef. Before the end of the day, we've put together two box sections and twenty-two honey frames. The last stage is to attach the flat rectangular wax foundations to the wire that runs through the frames. We do this with a special serrated wheel from Joseph's kit that, once heated a little, melts the wax onto the wire. Finally, we give a coat of white paint to all the outside surfaces of the box.

Tonight for their bedtime story the children hear extracts from *The Guide Book to Good Bee-Keeping*. I finish, 'And if the bees collect enough honey, we open the box and help ourselves,' although that very thought makes me shiver.

'And their babies?' the ever-thoughtful Alexandre asks.

'We have to leave enough honey to feed the babies to make more workers to make more honey,' I reply.

'Capitalist!' Anne shouts down from the cockpit.

Next morning the dinghy is fully loaded with 'bee gear', that is, the box sections, base, roof, combs, the smoker, industrial gloves, my coconut hat covered with a large piece of black mesh veil, long denim jeans from former non-tropical days, an even older denim fisherman's smock, and finally a pair of socks and sandals. Last, Anne passes down the 'live hive' which she is clearly relieved to see leave the boat.

I arrive on the reef at exactly the same moment as the morning lifeboat. As we all make our way across the reef to the shore, I have the strong feeling that I've rejoined the world's regular nine-to-five workforce. If the Russians are interested in my unusual bee gear, they don't show it. Like any busy commuters, we cross the reef absorbed in our private business and thoughts.

The place for the bees is behind the tank close to the biggest forest of coconut trees and a source of water. Now the moment of truth has arrived. I have to open the box and transfer the combs and bees to the main hive. In general, bees only bother me when they become entangled in my hair, but to purposely disturb a swarm of bees and move them about with no experience takes a certain reckless courage that is not my style.

'Cover up and use the smoker,' I remember Joseph saying as I dress up and put elastic bands around my gloves and the bottoms of my jeans. The black veil that I've tucked into my collar keeps popping out and I have to adopt the stiff-necked attitude of Frankenstein's monster as I move about. I wish now I could also adopt some of his indifferent confidence.

I lay out my only tool, a large screwdriver to pry out the combs; then I light the smoker. I take one last breath and look upward toward the heavens for courage. I find a group of Russians right behind me absolutely intent on what I'm doing. 'Back! Back! Bees, bees, bzzzzz, bzzzzz!' I shout in the manner of a tourist with local language problems. I then wave my arms about to frighten them away. They don't move and don't speak. One holds up a very old bellows-type camera and makes signs that he wants to take my photograph. I smile and pose for a moment, enjoying the popularity of a freak. I imagine the impact a photo of me in my crazy get-up will have on some family deep in the heart of Russia.

Puff, puff, I pump the smoker and slowly remove the top from the small hive. The bees are quiet, too quiet. In fact they are barely alive. Without problems I transfer the combs to the main hive. As the bees remain dormant, I can take my time to identify what looks like the wilting queen. My audience has fortunately moved on, so I can relax. I sit beside the hive until the first worker weakly staggers out from the front entrance of the hive to stretch his legs and look around his new workplace.

After a few days, the surviving bees have recuperated from their term of imprisonment. Each time I pass the hive, more and more workers make their daily sorties to return loaded down with pollen. Slowly but surely the hive establishes itself.

On the fourth day after our arrival all the visitors begin to break camp and move their equipment back to the boat. Greg has arranged a last-minute meeting for me with Katino on Ana-Ana. The Keplers are otherwise occupied in the general exodus.

For a Micronesian, Katino is quiet and serious. He tells me that the Keplers are so impressed with the pristine state of Caroline Atoll that they have decided to work toward protecting it as a bird sanctuary. He himself is interested in all our buildings and makes comparisons between my kitchen and that of a typical Polynesian house. It's a compliment, I know, but I'm a little disappointed that he hasn't noticed that I used a fairly sophisticated and original geometrical pattern for the design of the main frame. Perhaps he was only referring to the coconut leaf roof. I invite him aboard the boat to meet Anne and the children, but he says he has no time as the last lifeboat is waiting for him.

In the late afternoon *Akademik Korolev* disappears over the western horizon for the last time; no Russian scientists, no female defectors, no American biologists, no Katino. For a moment I suffer a sense of abandonment, which predictably passes as quickly as it came. Gradually the tension of human activity is replaced by the regular calm sounds of the island. I remind myself that this is where we have chosen to live and that we also have business to attend to.

Some years later I discover from a reputable source that *Akademik Korolev* was in truth one of Russia's primary spy ships. I don't know whether it was spying on Caroline or, if so, what for. Another day I also happen to read Katino's official report to the Kiribati government of 'The Visit of

Akademik Korolev to Caroline Atoll'. Our story takes up the last two pages of his report. He describes discovering a village and a meeting with a Scotsman who lives there with his French wife and two children. He continues with a description of the typical Polynesian domestic set-up, our arrangement with Captain Omer Darr and the fact that we have solar panels and transceiver radio capability. He ends:

> I found out that Falconer has a strong desire to stay and live on Caroline as long as he is permitted to. He loves living in isolation where he can relax and enjoy his life amidst the quietness and peacefulness of nature. He is a nature lover and I was led to believe this from the fact that Caroline Atoll has remained very much intact and unspoiled even though Falconer has been living there for quite some time.

> Katino Teebaki, Kiritimati. (Christmas Island)

15

Home Again

The wind blows strongly for a further three days. On the fourth day we decide to make a move to enter the pass. Anne is as desperate as I am to be back on the island, although she thinks the waves are bigger than they were the last time. They are certainly big. Once more we do battle with the turmoil of the seas just outside the pass before we surf wildly down the last wave to rush in through the entrance to the shocking calm of smooth tranquil waters inside the reef.

'The Napoleon fish is still here,' Alexandre comments as we make our way along the pass.

'And the turtle,' Anaïs adds. These animals are old friends by now – almost family.

Safely moored, we head straight for Ana-Ana. Alexandre as usual is the first to check out everything. 'Papa-Ya is dead,' he cries down to us while we're still unloading on the beach. He leads us to where Papa-Ya lies stiff and dry in a smoothed-out hollow hole.

'It looks like we missed a cockfight,' I say, trying to lighten the situation.

'I hope Omer is all right,' Anne worries, and immediately starts to chop coconuts and call in the hens.

Omer eventually limps into the clearing. Like an old war

veteran, he is followed by his admiring harem. His left foot is swollen and infected. Anne immediately takes him in hand and starts him on a course of antibiotic powders. After one week he returns to his old active self. Like a true hero, from then on he always retains his slight battle limp.

This year, along with our supplies, we've brought back a number of hundred-litre solid-metal food containers. Before closing their airtight lids on our precious food, we slip in a piece of cotton wool soaked in ether to suffocate any possible weevils hiding inside. The wheat we store in twenty-litre plastic jerry-cans with the same anti-weevil precaution.

In the garden I plant out the new banana shoots, as well as the breadfruit, mango and tamarind trees. The frangipani, hibiscus and flower of Tahiti cuttings I place around the house. For the first few days, the children stay close to the house. When they do eventually gather their old confidence and disappear to the beach, they return not long after with a collection of small plastic beads.

'Are these what the biologists were looking for?' Alexandre asks. His beads are about one-eighth of an inch in diameter and coloured yellow, blue, green and red.

'Could be,' I reply. 'Where did you find them?'

'All along the beach where the water finishes. They're mixed up amongst the coral. There are lots of them,' he explains.

I wonder what success, if any, the biologists had with their trawling and just how many of these little beads pollute our oceans for so many of them to arrive in this isolated spot so far from their source. For the next week the children's new game is 'The Biologists'. Their collection of beads grows daily and is methodically organised into separate containers for each colour.

The other new occupation for the children is school.

Last year Anne started nursery school for Alexandre and
Anaïs. They used *Petrel's* table, had small stools and drew
with coloured felt pens. They cut designs in paper, made
bead necklaces and generally had fun. This year Alexandre
has started a proper correspondence course, and everything
has changed. He struggles painfully with each new rigid
lesson. Anne, the professional, takes her time and searches
for ways to make the process easier. Still he finds it difficult
and generally ends up with his head on the table looking the
other way. The final breakdown comes when he starts
crying.

'Just leave him alone,' I argue with Anne. 'He's crying
because the effort to put things of no obvious interest into
his head is painful. I know all too well how that feels.'

'He has to learn to read, write and count,' she replies in
logical defence. 'It wouldn't be fair not to teach him that.'

'At what price?' I ask. 'You take an excited, observant
and contented child and break his spontaneity and intu-
ition by making him repeat "A B C D" one hundred times.
That's mental cruelty. When I was in school, I was part of
a big class and could rest way back in the last row. There
I would watch the teachers rave on while I stayed quiet with
my own busy thoughts. Alexandre has no choice or escape
with you always looking over his shoulder.'

'You can't just refuse to educate a child,' she insists.
'We live in the twentieth century. You give children an
education; then, at a certain age, they're free to choose what
they want to do. It's a duty.'

'I don't agree. Half of your so-called education is discipline and the training to make a child sit for hours in
a closed room. It's conditioning, brainwashing even, and
it's designed to prepare children to become obedient slaves
suitable to join the workers and support the capitalist
system. They end up no better than trained circus animals

that perform for rewards from their masters. As I see it, you're making a child's life miserable with a kind of training that isn't appropriate to his particular character, or to our particular situation here. We do live a long way from the mainstream of society, both physically and mentally.'

'You enjoy reading,' she argues. 'You use arithmetic in your navigation. What's the big difference?'

'I came late to reading and writing. It wasn't until I was in my thirties that I read all the school classics – and thoroughly enjoyed them. Mathematics and trigonometry I learned in night school when it was necessary for my architectural drawing work. I was by far the most attentive in our navigation class because I had a passion and a powerful motivation to learn. Alexandre is like me; he has his own sense of timing and priorities. He's observant and associates things well. His head is busy and content. He's just not ready to receive abstract learning symbols and irrelevant information.'

'You're not normal,' she replies.

'That's exactly my argument. A normal education didn't suit me, and it doesn't suit Alexandre. Just leave him alone for a while. He's smart enough to let us know what he wants and when he wants it. That would have been my ideal as a child.'

'Sometimes I think you came here just to prove to yourself and to the world that you are not in fact just plain stupid.'

'Not plain stupid, or just not plain normally stupid – you choose. But if either is right, it's all the more reason to take care to avoid giving Alexandre any possible hang-ups about his learning abilities.' I'm being stubborn, I know, since this subject is close to my heart. However, I acknowledge that schooling is Anne's domain, just as house-building was mine.

Anne sincerely examines her reasoning. She wants to do what is right. After reflection, though, she can't break away from her schoolteacher's mentality and instilled sense of educational responsibility. Alexandre's tears continue. Anaïs doesn't help since, although she is two years Alexandre's junior, she, like Anne, has absolutely no problem in absorbing any kind of information. She can remember and repeat almost every last detail of all of Alexandre's lessons.

While Anne and I disagree about the more formal aspects of the children's education, we are in complete agreement about the informal benefits of living on Caroline. We see the many rich, unique and valuable experiences the children have each day within our tight and secure family unit. The space they have to explore creative ideas keeps them passionately occupied. Their many opportunities for adventurous exploration are kept within their physical and mental limitations.

Now that we're back on the island I have a new problem: the wheat grinder. In general, the new wheat flour is a great success. It gives our bread and crepes a richer and sweeter taste. The difficulty is that it takes over thirty minutes to grind enough flour for each baking. For a while I justify the chore by recognising its muscle-building potential. Very soon my vain image of Mr Universe tires, though, and I look for some more sensible alternative.

'A windmill,' I say. 'That's the way they used to grind the grain. The power of the wind to turn the grinder to produce the flour.'

'What about the "no technology" thing?' Anne, the alert purist, reminds me.

'A windmill is different. There's something mystical and poetic about using the power of the wind, like the sails on the boat and *Mini-Mini*. It all fits in with the solar and quiet reusable energy principle.'

'All right, but where do you find materials?' she queries.

'For the main centre piece I can use that old axle on South Islet. Then, the biologists left some long galvanised tubes. I can tie them onto the wheel and make long sail-like wings from the old spinnaker material on the boat. All I really have to do is build a large frame to hold the main axle.'

Making the frame structure adjustable to the wind presents too much of a mechanical problem. I settle for a fixed frame similar to that used to hold logs for sawing, only higher. I rely on the regularity and fixed direction of the trade winds.

My building projects have used up every last Nono tree on Ana-Ana, so an expedition to Puti-Puti is required before the large frame can stand high and proud on our small beach. To retrieve the axle, I take *Mini-Mini* to South Islet. The only way I can load the axle is to tip the dinghy on its side and roll the wheels aboard. With a block and tackle from the boat plus some difficult levering, the heavy axle finally sits in place on Ana-Ana, rising fully nine feet above the ground. Tying on the tubes is pretty straightforward. For a start I make sails for only two of the four blades, which measure fourteen feet from tip to tip.

'Just hold it steady till I fit the other sail,' I say to Anne as, even with only one sail attached, the windmill is ready to take off.

'You've created a dangerous monster,' she comments, while she struggles to hold back its impressive power.

'It's better than a muscle-bound monster,' I say. 'Besides, it's progress or no bread.'

When I finally let the blade fly away from my tight grasp, Anne is a long way back, fearfully guarding the children and dog. Swoosh, swoosh, swoosh – it's magnificent! Quickly it settles to a regular rhythm of around one revolution per second.

'Super!' the children cry and clap their hands in total delight. We watch it for a while in pleased contentment – until I realise I now have to stop it. I slip in behind the blades and with great difficulty eventually succeed in jamming a piece of wood between the wheel and the frame to slow the blades back down to a nervous stop.

In front of the wheel I build a solid shelf to support the grinder and attach its turning arm through the spokes of the wheel. I place an inverted bottle of wheat into the tiny hopper of the grinder and set a tin below to collect the ground flour. The last refinement is a quick-release arrangement of the sails for easy stopping. Each time I grind wheat, our little windmill takes on an air of fantasy. Its white flashing wings encourage us to follow the ways of the day as fancy free as leaves, blown along in the wind.

For how long can we guard our isolated world? That is my preoccupation. The scientific expedition was a surprise. How many more expeditions or adventurers can we expect to interfere with our magic high-flying world and bring it crashing down to the ground? 'For how long?' I breathe into the slow-turning sails of our windmill. Then I listen intently for the slightest whispered indication from the 'swish, swish' of its fairy wings. 'Take care, take care,' it murmurs. 'Take care.'

16

Guardians of Everything

We have reached the point where the continual activities of establishing our place here have settled into a balanced routine. We're the loving guardians of our total environment, including ourselves. I look around Caroline and realise I've found a place of peace – my treasure of the South Pacific. All my sailing, cruising and observing have found a focus here. This is the climax of a long and passionate love affair with my boat, the sea and isolated islands.

In an atmosphere of calm I've had the opportunity to sort through many of the unanswered questions that always clogged up the back of my mind and weren't fully resolved in my solitary life on the boat. Surrounded by, and interacting with, pure nature in myriad forms, I've discovered that profound place within myself that is the centre of all my anxieties and sensitivities, and I've come to acknowledge the voice of my innocent inner self. My own common sense has developed into a freedom and openness to accept almost anything, from nature's surprises to the arrival of diverse visitors. Through this experience I have learned how to balance priorities while avoiding becoming trapped – of having fun and, hopefully, always moving towards an optimal way of life.

In peace I have cleared my mind of the clutter of outward

experiences to discover the huge depth of experience within that works for each of us like a guardian angel. With practice and reflection, I've learned how to interact with this profound friend, even when separated from the physical presence of Caroline. I now feel freer to express my innermost thoughts.

'This is it,' I say to Anne in one of my high moments.

'*What* is it?' she asks, a little bewildered.

'Everything we have here – an island, a house, enough food and water…'

'Those are all material comforts,' she interrupts. 'What about your famous art of living?'

'My art of living is the most important of all! It's simply feeling good. If we surround ourselves with things we love, we feel good.'

'That's not always easy,' she says thoughtfully.

'Trying is what it's all about,' I conclude.

I'm really surprised one day when Alexandre asks, 'Is god real?' So far, the only mythical figure to visit Caroline has been Santa Claus. He must have heard about god back on Ahe.

'Different people believe in different gods,' I answer slowly. 'Each one says his god is the real one and will even fight to defend his or her particular god.'

'Why?' he asks quickly.

'Well, it's important to think that what you believe is true. Like if someone told you Mummy was not your real mummy, you would be upset.'

'But she is our real mummy.' Anaïs's reaction is fast and tears form in her eyes.

'How could she not be our real mummy?' Alexandre asks.

'Well, you could be someone else's baby that she now takes care of.'

'That's not true, Mummy is our mummy,' Anaïs insists.

I sense that our discussion is veering off track. 'Yes, Mummy is your mummy, but you see it's important for you that it's really true.'

'So which god is really true?' Alexandre persists.

'Well,' I hesitate, 'maybe they're all true or maybe none of them are true.'

'I don't understand,' he says, watching me closely for my reply.

'Well, *something* makes everything,' I begin with a shrug of my shoulders.

'You said that things just happen over a long, long time,' Alexandre recalls.

'Well, that's the way I see it; that's what I believe.'

'So is that a god?' he asks, still concentrating on my reaction.

'If we want we can make a god of time and happenings. Yes.'

'But it wouldn't be real,' he replies.

'If we really believe that a universal force brings everything together over a long period of time, and that action creates things, then we could call that force god and it would be real,' I finish, not sure that he really follows my explanation.

On Caroline I have the opportunity to see clear evidence of this strong creative force, which is consistent and runs through all things we can perceive. Its action produces all sorts of glorious beauty in our world – the touch of a loving mate, the symphony of singing birds, the blossoming of a sweet-smelling flower or the moon in its phases. Yet it's the interaction of these creations that produces what we see as tragic or sad in our world, be it the pain of violence or sickness or a frigate bird eating a newly born turtle.

If you're a busy individual, infinitely creative in all senses of the word, and opportunistic and expansionist when it comes to ensuring personal survival, then it could be said that you are a good representative of the force that holds the universe together. You can, if you wish, lay all the responsibilities for your particular character and actions at the feet of this same force that, for better or for worse, through evolution, created you in its own complex image.

Belonging to a civilised society involves being part of a group of people – a village or a nation, for example – who have agreed to live according to certain generalised principles of behaviour and who have evolved a common mentality, which includes personal discipline, behavioural patterns, codes, morals, ethics and even religious beliefs. These beliefs, as often as not, are at war with the creative force and our basic natures. As individuals, we find it difficult to control our inner forces and come to terms with the often conflicting and confusing disciplines of organised society. Mostly we try – sincerely joining this brave human experiment – to find a way to reconcile these conflicts.

This effort always has the potential to go astray. Greed-driven political pressures can easily progress along dangerous paths and develop ways to threaten our overall survival. As individuals, we must remain wary and active, using our common sense against these deviations that poison our environment and quality of life. We must never forget that our new game is still full of all the possible nuances of human behaviour, and that the original jungle code will always be present just behind the theatrical interaction of everyday living. There the force rests – mostly under control but always with the possibility of reverting to its own ways, one of which is to cheat the established rules and make others its victims.

The nearest our family has come to any religious ritual here is that we've created our own special Sun Days. Here in the tropics, the sun passes directly over Caroline twice a year, once on its journey north and then again on its journey south. With the aid of the nautical almanac, we find the two days of the year when the sun's declination is exactly ten degrees south of the equator (October and February). Then with a vertical nail on a supported horizontal board, we wait for midday when the shadow of the nail forms a small circle around itself. At this special moment, with the sun directly overhead and looking down on the island, I make my speech: 'Welcome, Sun, once more to our little island. Thank you for your light, your warmth and for making our lives possible. We wish you a long life, a good onward journey and look forward to your faithful return.'

'Why do you talk to the sun?' Anaïs asks.

'And to the boat, the wind and the sea?' Alexandre adds.

'And to the sharks, the fish and the birds?' Anaïs continues.

'I suppose,' I begin, 'it's because we are all part of everything and I like to feel close to everything around me. I talk first, then listen, as I do with you.'

'Things don't talk,' Anaïs states defiantly.

'Everything has its own way of communicating,' I try to explain. 'If we listen very carefully with all our senses, we can perhaps understand what they're saying.'

'Things don't talk,' Anaïs repeats with the same conviction. Smiling, I give up trying to convince her.

'With all your philosophising, I don't know how these children are ever going to adjust to a normal society,' Anne sniffs.

'Normal society,' I respond, 'is only another kind of religion. It gives direction and motivation to an animal that will cling to any form of established belief in an attempt to escape the abyss of confusion. The most important thing to me is that the children are comfortable with who and what they are themselves. Then they'll be capable of adapting to any kind of society or religion that suits them.'

'How did you ever end up such a dreamer?' Anne asks sincerely.

'For me, that question is back to front. Once you acknowledge the limitations of our few senses, our profound fears, the prejudices acquired by experience, our particular blind spots, plus the anticipation of our own death, I question all our logical attempts at reasoning with ourselves. In fact, I've come to the conclusion that we're all dreamers who live in our own personal fantasy world, which we then call reality. It's this personal world view that forms all our personal priorities, and raises in us all our questions. All the paths you chase through life have only one real destination: to satisfy the source that created the questions, which of course is you yourself.'

'LIFE – a personal problem,' she sighs.

'Finally, yes, life is a personal problem, or rather a personal concern, and once you accept this,' I counter, 'really accept your personal dream state with all its nuances, take time to enter it, always to confront its questions, while not forgetting the dark creator down in the basement who is obliged to keep the fire burning...' I take a deep breath – 'then things become very interesting and intense. Then you can contact the full power that is you and touch your true inner self and, like when you're making love, really begin to fly.'

'My dream state is a busy logical mind that won't shut down,' Anne muses. 'Even alone in the jungle, I still count each coconut as I put it in my sack.'

'And making love?' I ask innocently

'Well, I'm not counting,' she laughs.

I've long lost count of the production of our papaya trees. I do know that we are now eating so many papayas each day that the palms of our hands and the soles of our feet have turned a distinct shade of yellow. After being brought up in a country where getting drunk is almost a national sport, I have one criterion against which I defend most of my unusual activities: 'It is better than sitting in the pub.' Nevertheless, from time to time I enjoy a glass of wine. When I left Scotland, I added a slim volume to my onboard library called *How to Make Your Own Wine*. I decide to put the information in this book to practical use.

First, I make a thick juice from some ripe papayas, then add sugar, a teaspoon of bread yeast and enough warm water to fill up one of the gallon demijohn bottles from the beach. A small plastic tube and cork forms an air lock. With the warm temperature of the tropics it's not long before the brew begins to ferment. In our simplicity this continual move-ment of escaping bubbles becomes as entertaining as a TV show. We eat our meals against the background of the steady plop, plop, plop of escaping gas.

Two local lizards have also become mesmerised by the fermenting process and spend their days as faithful patrons of Caroline's only pub. There they remain all day in a long alcoholic haze, sustained only by the odd drop of escaping sugary mixture. After fourteen days the fermentation finishes, and the lizards stagger back home to their loved ones to sober up. Now it's the turn of the winemakers. For a perfect wine it's too fresh and a bit too sweet. After per-sistent tests, however, there is no doubt about its alcoholic content.

'It's for our visitors,' I explain to two slightly mystified children.

'Is George coming back?' Alexandre wants to know.

'No, it's Olivier and Lawrence. You remember we met them on their yacht *Iferouane* in Moorea.'

'And they're coming here?' Alexandre suggests.

'We're not sure yet, but they telephoned Les and want to contact us by radio.'

Olivier and Lawrence are French, both teachers and experienced ocean sailors. They live aboard their own comfortable, fast aluminium yacht, using their transceiver radio as Bernard does his engine – only when absolutely necessary.

'Ron, I have problems hearing you,' Olivier repeats as he makes his best effort to tune his radio and at the same time speak good English. I have difficulties pulling his faint words out of the background static. I understand eventually only that they want to come and visit us for their Christmas holidays. He adjusts something and finally his voice comes booming in loud and clear, and we can have a normal conversation.

'Is there anything we can bring you?' he asks brightly.

'Well, yes, Olivier, if possible you could bring us all our mail and Christmas parcels that Omer is holding.'

'No problems, Ron – anything else?'

I know Olivier is a champion at finding fruit, either growing wild or on disused property, so I say, 'Well, anything fresh and eatable would be appreciated.'

'No problems, Ron,' he repeats. 'Anything else?'

I'm not prepared for all his enthusiasm to act as a transport ship and hesitate for a moment. Lately I've been thinking about the possibilities of building a large ferro-concrete water tank close to the house. It would hold around 2500 litres and solve all our water problems. I've even reached the point of making a list of materials. Now I try to imagine a long bundle of rusting reinforcing bars lying on *Iferouane*'s immaculate deck, and cement dust settling on the rows of bound books below, and wonder where he would store a full roll of chicken wire.

'What about some cement, reinforcing bars and chicken

wire?' I say, with an apologetic 'I can only ask' shrug to Anne.

'No problems,' he replies immediately. 'How many bags of cement, what size of re-bar and how much chicken wire?'

I smile at Anne and whisper, 'That's the tank started.'

Iferouane arrives one week before Christmas. The weather is moderate. I can easily row out of the pass entrance to meet them in the open sea. The first thing I notice as they help me aboard is the large rust stain that runs from the bundle of bars clear down to the stern of their boat. On the other side of the deck a bulky roll of chicken wire blocks up the passageway.

'Keep a little left of centre,' I advise him quietly as the entrance of the pass approaches, 'and be prepared to turn a little to the right at the last moment.'

Olivier remains cool, concentrating. I feel the lift of the last wave, and we plunge in from the wild open sea to the peaceful calm of the pass without problems.

'Welcome to Caroline,' I reply to Lawrence's relieved smile from the bow.

The most impressive thing about our visitors is their power and energy. Without taking a break they have all the plastic-covered cement bags out on deck and loaded into *Mini-Mini*. By the end of the morning, all the materials have been brought ashore and together we've constructed a special shelf under the kitchen roof to spread out all the sackfuls of grapefruit and lemons they have brought. By the end of the day they have seen every last thing on Ana-Ana, made a tour of South Island and visited *Petrel*, the bees and the cistern. The day after, they walk around the full ring of Caroline's thirty-nine islets, a distance of fourteen miles, then still have the energy when they return to go out on the reef at night to hunt lobsters.

Christmas dinner includes grilled lobster, pumpkin pie,

cucumber, tomato and heart-of-palm salad, and a special grapefruit dessert, all washed down with sweet fresh papaya wine.

Santa is helped out this year with presents for the children from their Taddy and Granny in Paris, which includes some gold and silver tinsel that we use to decorate the house.

After the New Year our visitors regretfully return to their university jobs. For us, their visit has been agreeable and stimulating, and with the materials they brought we have the beginning of our new tank.

17

The Concrete and the Symbolic

'Ferroconcrete,' I reply to Anne's usual questioning of my projects. 'They build boats that way. You build a steel frame, cover it with layers of chicken wire, then plaster on concrete.'

'Have you ever made anything like that before?' she questions.

'No, but first times are fun,' I reply with a laugh.

The children help to collect sand from the beach with their small buckets. We mix the cement into a paste on a large solid piece of beachcombed plywood. Soon the concrete base is finished. I form a steel frame five feet wide by seven feet high on this foundation with a narrow bottle-type opening on top. We wrap the chicken wire around and around the frame and wire it to the bars.

When it comes to the plastering, unfortunately the mesh isn't dense enough to hold the soft plaster. We have to place shuttering boards inside and out as a support for our muddy concrete mix. Day after day, with lots of hammering on the boards to remove the trapped air bubbles and lots of laughter, the tank slowly grows. I don't forget to set in two galvanised pipes, one for the supply tap and one on the bottom for a drain.

'This tank is going to be here for a very long time,' I say to my workers.

'How long?' Alexandre asks.

'A hundred years, maybe two hundred – anyway, it will still be here long after we're gone.'

'Where are we going?' Anaïs asks.

'Nowhere for the moment, but concrete tanks live longer than people. I want to leave something on Caroline that will still be here many years from now.'

'Like the baby's tombstone,' Alexandre suggests, referring to the sad little marker we found on South Islet.

'Yes, just like a tombstone,' I agree, not knowing then how close to the truth his comparison would prove to be. 'We're all going to put something on the tank that will explain to future people how and why we lived here.'

'Why *do* we live here?' Alexandre asks thoughtfully.

'Because this is the best place in the whole world that I've found to live in peace and quiet,' I answer as Anne blows out her cheeks in exasperation at my repeated idealist pretensions.

'We have a little time before the final cement coat goes hard,' I continue, 'so find a sharp nail and we'll start drawing.'

The tank, for no reason other than the idiosyncrasies of the builder, who is tuned in to the world's magnetic forces, is oriented north, south, east and west, as is everything else on Ana-Ana. I begin our legend by drawing on each of the four compass corners the heads of three Polynesian gods (tikis).

'Why three?' asks Anaïs, who has been sitting on the ground watching the artist at work.

'Well, the top one is looking up to the clouds to call the rain,' I start, trying now to analyse logically what I've just created intuitively. I develop my theme: 'The bottom one is looking down to the ground to help the things grow.'

'And the middle one?' Alexandre has to inquire.

'Ah! The middle one is watching us, to make sure that we use the rain, the ground and everything here in an appropriate way.'

'What can we do wrong?' Alexandre asks sincerely.

'Caroline became beautiful on her own and will continue to stay beautiful on her own. We must do nothing to change that.'

'Like the animals,' Alexandre suggests philosophically.

'Like the animals and the plants,' Anne mimics.

I mark off two areas, one on each side of the tap, for the young designers. They are ready, but hesitate until they see what I'm going to do. On the north side I draw a sketch of *Fleur d'Ecosse* and *Mini-Mini*.

'That's our transport,' I say. 'Now I'm going to draw all the buildings.'

Anne fills the south side of the tank with an abstract symbolic sketch of the island. She draws in two adults, two children, a dog, a cat, two parakeets, fish, a coconut crab, a lobster and finally the sun and the moon. When I question some mysterious dots in one corner, I am quickly informed, 'Those are the bees.'

Alexandre, on the other hand, has drawn a typical modern town house with normal frame windows and a chimney that he has taken straight from his western schoolbooks. Anaïs has filled her square like her mother, with abstract symbolic lines that no doubt make sense to her, but which I fear will be a great puzzle to future visitors.

Along with all our names and dates of birth I copy out a short poem I wrote earlier:

Children lost in the Universe,
Playing all the games they dare.
Millionaires of the moment,
Rich in what isn't there.

What our tank's markings will say to future explorers of Caroline I can only guess. What our drawings say to me is quite significant. My tikis of the elements speak of my need for courage and understanding to support the rather fragile circumstances in which we find ourselves. They represent my external guardian angels who communicate directly with my personal guardian angel within. Symbolic images we use to communicate with the spiritual world, they could be compared to the symbolic everyday words we use to communicate with each other, and associate with our material and abstract thoughts.

The children's drawings also intuitively represent their own worlds of understanding. Anne's drawings represent her more practical approach to her surroundings. Her stick figures and scattered representations of the material aspects of our lives are reminiscent of old Indian drawings.

Those sketches on the concrete walls of Caroline's tank could be compared to drawings made by ancient cave-dwellers or the modern graffiti proliferating on subway walls and tenement halls. All tell a particular human story, indicating significant priorities and reflecting day-to-day lives at a particular time in our short history. Our story speaks specifically of a period near the end of the twentieth century when a small family belonging to the space age travelled on a long journey, far from the madding crowd, to find themselves alongside the plants and animals. There, communicating in their humble way with the wind, rain, soil and sun, they grew close to the force of nature, and moved in sympathetic harmony with all creation.

Next day we finish off the inside of the tank. I can stand fully upright as I methodically plaster over all the imperfections left by the shuttering boards. It's cool inside the tank. When we talk our voices echo from the walls. This initiates a new game: we make long mantra-type droning sounds that reverberate and resound as they would from monastery walls.

'You know, I have another use for this tank,' I confide to my fellow meditators during a brief interlude from our absorption in the enclosed world.

'What's that?' Anaïs asks, coming out of her reverie.

'Well, if we ever get a big cyclone here, when the trees are falling and the house is being blown away, what are we going to do?' I wait for a response.

'We're going to climb in here, shut the hole on top and wait until it's all over,' Alexandre suggests.

'Right, first we drain out all the water, then put in food, water, clothes, our tools and the radio, then Kiki, Dou-Dou and the birds. We all wait inside until the storm passes.'

Anaïs, being practical and observant in her mother's style, takes a slow look around the small enclosed space, then comments, 'There's not going to be much room.'

We'll consider that another day. For the moment the tank is ready. We eagerly await the next rainfall.

Anne's passion is collecting interesting bottles from the beach. A considerable pyramid of empties, dedicated to Alcoholics Anonymous, has accumulated close to the house. The bottles are square, round and triangular in shape and vary in colour from transparent to jet black. Most represent well-known makes like Glenfiddich and Bell's whisky, as well as wines from every corner of the globe. With the small amount of cement left from the tank, I have an idea about how to make use of these reminders of good times past.

'So, you want to use my precious bottles to build a new concrete barbecue,' Anne sums up my proposal with some protest.

'You'll be able to admire their wonderful bottoms for the rest of your days,' I tempt her sexual sensibility.

Unable to find a reason to say no, Anne reluctantly agrees to let me use her fine collection of possible antiques for artistic purposes. First, the old coral barbecue is cleared away. Working as usual as a team, we start by laying down a circle of concrete. Carefully and precisely we arrange a circular row of 'bottoms-out' bottles and press them into the cement. Round and round we go, first a layer of cement and then the bottles. My assistants are enthusiastic about their choice of best bottoms.

Our barbecue, a permanent monument to the inebriation of our species and decadent times, ends up four feet in diameter and three feet high. It is made from a selection of 192 bottles representing the top international brands.

Our lives continue to rotate around the natural phases of each day. Although in general we adopt the simpler behavioural patterns of our less distracted cousins, the animals and plants, our active imaginations and inventive minds regularly tempt us to complicate our lives. These impulses, although less frequent as time goes on, still pop up occasionally to divert us from the simple way. I prefer, for the moment, to let these passions express themselves. Then, with use and experience, we test them in our rigorous Quality Control department. For example, taking a shower on Caroline at first consists of scooping up water from a bowl or bucket and pouring it over your head. 'What we lack is a proper shower,' I declare.

'What we lack is all modern conveniences,' Anne points out. 'I thought that was the idea.'

'I mean a solar shower,' I say, defending my newest inspiration, 'and that's permissible.'

'With you writing your own personal song of life,' she says, 'everything is permissible.'

'It's an open trial-and-error melody, the evolution of quality culture,' I philosophise.

The large black plastic buoy we found on Nake Islet forms the main body of the shower – the tank. I cut out a filling hole on top and another hole in the bottom, into which I screw a brass tap. When it's half full of water, I can just hoist it above our heads using the block and tackle from the boat. By sunset the water inside is really hot. For a while we all delight in the pleasure of a civilised overhead hot running shower. After a few weeks, however, the chore of filling and hoisting this heavy container becomes more of a burden than a delight. This aspect of civilisation is referred to the Quality Control department, where it is carefully re-examined by the inventor and marked down as one more good thing which proved to be not so good.

When I bake bread or use the oven, it's necessary to keep the fast-burning coconut husks constantly under control. To fill the periods between stoking I practise my harmonica. With constant repetition I make some real progress. In time I build a small repertoire of Scottish folk songs, sea shanties and songs of the sixties. I can even throw in a little jazzy improvisation to fill out the melodies.

Confident with my harmonica progress, I experiment by attaching the harmonica to the top of my autoharp. Now, not only can I play the melodies, I can at the same time accompany myself with chords and rhythm. The amazing one-man band is born. I make progress until I can easily close my eyes and drift into that hypnotic trance common to all true performers.

My inner visions vary. I begin all alone on the stage of the biggest stadium in the world. I play sweetly and emotionally to touch the very soul and mesmerise my audience of thousands. My repertoire is entirely made up of original songs that celebrate nature. In song, I share my philosophies, observations and inspirations along with the joys and difficulties of being alive. I become a cult figure at the forefront of a new natural lifestyle movement.

This bubble pops as I stoke up the fire. I settle for one of my more attainable dreams: the life of a busker. Dedicated to my free music I busk alone in the marketplaces of the big cities of the world. I play appropriate themes amid the sounds of the street to a passing public, waiting for someone to throw me a coin for my next meal.

Carried away by the musical world and my abstract visions, I take my one-man band out onto the beach, to play for the whispering spirits of the gods. I begin with the sunset and improvise fading melodies to accompany the soft dying colours of the slowly setting orange sun. My themes are calm and pleasing, and I breathe quietly and deeply.

Suddenly I'm caught by an active drama taking place over the lagoon. For a while I just sit and watch. It's the big frigate birds who normally keep to themselves as they confidently soar on the trade wind. Now, in preying pairs, they await the return of the boobies, who have spent their day fishing far out at sea. The frigates single out a particular booby, then proceed to chase it up, down and around until either it escapes or it is panicked into throwing up its undigested catch of the day. This is what the frigates have anticipated. They immediately leave their victim to swoop down over the lagoon and intercept the falling fish before it hits the water.

These World-War-I style aerial dogfights excite me and give inspiration to a new kind of agitated melody. In the tradition of the old silent movie organists I adapt my accompaniment to accentuate the mounting tension, the attack, the wild chase and the big finish of this live theatre performance. I support the underdog and hate the aggressor. Sadly, it usually ends with glory for the villain and tragedy for the victim.

I am soon cast in the role of the aggressor myself, as I have to plunder honey from the bees. Four months have passed since their installation. Each time I visit the hive, I've seen a steady flow of exiting workers and a constant stream of returning pollen-laden pirates. The only improvement to my bee gear is that my veil fits better and allows me to exhibit a little less Frankenstein-like movement.

Puff, puff, my old panic sets in as I nervously lift off the roof and top cover to add smoke. The response is a deep, ominous, defensive hum from the centre of the swarm. When I apply more smoke in and around the combs, the hum deepens into a threatening groan of possible action by the masses. In total fear I pry out one of the centre combs. It's heavy and full of honey. It's also covered with hundreds of bees.

I repeat Joseph's instructions out loud: 'Give the comb a sharp blow against the hand and the bees will fall off.' It doesn't work. The bees hang on as if their lives depended on it and are obviously very annoyed by this rough treatment. 'Another possibility is to brush them off with a bunch of grass,' Joseph had said. We have no grass here.

I grab a piece of coconut leaf and begin to persuade the desperate, united workforce to leave their workplace. One by one they let go, only to regroup over my head. Now I'm really sweating. Once again I seriously question my sanity as I prepare to confront a foreign queen along with her faithful fanatical followers. Blind concentration, coupled with fear and determination, enables me to remove all the full honeycombs from the open hive and replace them with empty combs. All the while the buzzing increases around my head until there are so many bees clinging to my veil that I have difficulty seeing anything at all.

As I finally refit the roof, I feel the first sting through my socks. Then the bees begin to attack my arms through my light smock. In panic I begin an adrenaline-assisted run, away from the hive, through the trees and out past the amazed expressions of Anne and the children. The bees are still following me as I cross the beach and run far out onto the dry reef. I fling my arms around my head like a windmill. At the edge of the reef I hesitate before diving into shark-infested water, then discover, to my extreme relief, that the bees have gone. All that remains is my throbbing heart and the painful swellings on my arms and feet.

My audience, once they realise my condition is not fatal, have some difficulty keeping straight faces. All the way back to the house they repeat the story over and over again in increasing detail: how many bees there were around my head, how fast I was running and how at first they didn't even know what was happening. The pain eases during the afternoon. Together we break the honey-filled wax combs into a big bowl made from a plastic buoy neatly cut in two. Through a piece of cotton we filter out the dark golden honey until we have filled five large coffee jars (10 kg). This honey has its own unique taste. We ceremoniously label it 'Caroline's Coconut Blossom Honey'.

We have available for our table several kinds of fish: a large trigger fish with a thick, solid skin and a taste that is more like lamb or veal than fish, a small silver oily fish that reminds me of a Scottish herring, and a grouper that tastes like cod. There are parrotfish, red snappers, rainbow runners and various small lagoon fish – each with its own taste and all good to eat. Sometimes we bring in a tuna or mahi-mahi. Often we eat coconut crabs, shellfish or octopus. If we have the energy, lobsters are available out on the open reef for the taking. All of these we can boil, fry, barbecue, bake or eat raw with vinegar and sauces. We make fresh coconut milk all the time, as it is excellent with every kind of fish. Often we barbecue a complete fish over the ashes of the fire. Then we carefully pick the meat away from the bone with our fingers. When she has a good catch, Anne cuts extra fillets that we dry in the sun. This ends up as a kind of fish jerky that we can store away for a stormy day.

Eventually Anne begins to weary of fishing every single day, and it's time to introduce the idea of a fish trap to ensure a steady supply for our table. The only possible place I have found so far for a fish trap on Caroline is the small pass that we use for *Mini-Mini*, which connects the lagoon and Blind Passage. We've already deepened this pass. Now we build two low walls of coral to form a diversion that funnels into a pool alongside the pass. At the end of the funnel we place a fairly large mesh basket.

Together we surround a shoal of white parrotfish that have been feeding in the shallow water over the reef. With lots of shouting and splashing we herd them towards the trap. Kiki brings any escapees back. Most of the panicked fish dash desperately away during the final closing-in stage, but a few enter our trap. I lift the basket out of the water and high over my head. We enjoy an instant shower provided by at least a dozen large parrotfish who thrash around in the bottom of the basket. We have enough fish for the day.

We leave the basket in place with the idea that, when we come back the following day, it will again be filled with fresh fish. But when we arrive the next morning, all that remains of our basket is a tightly twisted ball of mesh. I imagine that, after devouring all the trapped fish, some attacking sharks ended up fighting over the basket itself.

While we try to salvage something from this bundle of steel wire, Kiki decides to chase one of the guilty marauding sharks who pass close by. Despite her short legs, she makes good speed leaping through the shallow water over the flat open reef. With loud barks she tries hard to corner her panicked victim. Unfortunately, a bigger shark, attracted by the action, begins to chase Kiki. Afraid for Kiki's safety, I run after the second shark, throwing pieces of coral and shouting at the top of my voice to attract its attention. The chase continues around and around the reef until the second shark gives up. Then Kiki drives her victim into shallow water and drags it by the dorsal fin up onto the dry reef.

One less shark will change our situation very little. Much to Kiki's annoyance, and thanks to my sense of oneness-with-life, I grab the thrashing shark by the tail and drag it back into deep water. While I catch my breath, I wonder with amusement if shark-chasing could ever be developed into an Olympic sport.

Most afternoons I take the children swimming in our special pool that lies between two of the islets close by Ana-Ana. Alexandre can already swim; now it's Anaïs's turn to learn the 'doggy paddle', the style common to all Polynesian children. She is not at all afraid and already pushes herself clear off the bottom for a few strokes at a time. Swimming time develops into playtime. We invent complicated games with boats and pirates, building larger and larger driftwood rafts for our ships. Mostly for the interest of 'Pap', we have races with small boats made from half coconuts. First I fix on a heavy metal centre keel then load on as much sail as I think the little tubs will carry. I arrange the sails so that they will self-steer. With cheering and encouraging calls we race these 'hot rods' down the full length of the pool.

Caroline's ability to collect rubbish from all over the world is not reflected in our settlement. Our contribution to the trash market is practically nil. Our few precious tin cans are cleaned and put aside for future planting out of seeds, measuring rainfall, building sandcastles or as containers for anything from nails to shells. Any paper is carefully kept dry under the house for lighting fires. All the rest is simply organic and is devoured by the dog, cat, hens, birds, lizards, cockroaches or ants.

In an attempt to improve the growing qualities of the garden soil, which remains poor, I create a fish-sauce fertiliser by filling a large container with leftover fish and leaving it to decompose. It turns into such a strong live bacteria acid that I have to be careful my hands are not dissolved as I work with the brew. Before using it on the garden I have to dilute it many times over. Needless to say, the smell is terrible.

'We came all this way only to end up breathing the fumes of a rotten-fish factory,' Anne complains.

I have to agree with her. We put it to Quality Control, where it is decided that nose welfare wins over plant welfare. Another potentially good idea evaporates into thin air.

Our daily bread is also our daily newspaper. At each baking I carefully scratch out on each loaf the headlines of the day's big events: 'Rain', 'More chicks', 'Watermelon', 'Happy Easter', 'New moon', 'Lobster', 'Fish trap', 'Sharks', 'Fish sauce', or whatever. My readers are faithful and never fail to show great interest in the editor's interpretation of the priorities of each passing day.

The weeks pass easily, marked by the books we read, a shower of rain, the changing phases of the moon. The 'rat count' has grown to an impressive 1089. The ants, who have been raked over, stood on, burnt out and just generally discouraged, are no longer a real problem. I have also systematically searched the whole of Ana-Ana for any possible trapped water where mosquitoes could breed. I even went so far as to cut deep grooves in all the trees to drain away any pools that formed between the branches after a shower of rain. The end result is that the mosquitoes, who anyway were never numerous, have all but disappeared.

Our second year is coming to a close. We begin to tune in regularly to Arnold, a radio operator on Rarotonga in the Cook Islands, who transmits detailed weather information daily for yachts sailing throughout the South Pacific. One day he has a personal message for us. After my call sign he asks, 'What's happening to your quiet paradise island, Ron?'

'All's well here, Arnold – what do you mean?'

'Yes, well, I just found something in our local paper here, the *Cook Island News*. Find a pencil and I'll read it to you.'

Anne has overheard the conversation and now comes to the radio.

'Go ahead, Arnold.'

'It's a short news item on Caroline Island. It says: "The Kiribati government has given a French Polynesian businessman approval for a hotel and fishing venture on the distant Caroline and Flint Islands. Mr Alex Orama has proposed the building of hotels on the two islands and the creation of a fishing industry to export marine produce to Tahiti."' As we pause in shocked silence, he says, 'How's the copy so far, Ron?'

'Good copy, Arnold. I'm just surprised, carry on.'

'Yes, I can understand that,' he answers quietly, hesitating as if he would rather not be the one passing on this news. He continues: '"The Kiribati foreign investment officer, Itintaake Etuati, said that, under a draft agreement, the Kiribati government will give Mr Orama a fifty-year lease to govern land on both islands, with a review of rental every five years. The project is expected to employ eighty to one hundred Kiribati nationals." That's about it, Ron. It looks like you could be in for some company.'

'We know nothing at all about this. I have to say it all sounds a little extraordinary and a bit of wishful thinking on Orama's part.'

'Well, anyway, I thought you'd be interested. Good luck, Ron. I'll get on with my weather report.'

'Omer has lost his lease!' Anne cries immediately. 'We'll have to leave!'

'We don't know how true it is,' I say quietly, a little surprised at her panic at the thought of having to leave the island. But it's true that with time Anne has come to love Caroline as her island. Here she is queen, and she knows it. 'Wait until we get back to Moorea,' I insist. 'Then we'll check it out with Omer. If worst comes to worst, maybe we can make an arrangement with this Mr Alex Orama.'

'You really want to stay here and be part of a large commercial complex?' she asks.

'A commercial development here is not at all obvious to me. The world is full of dreamers. I refuse to believe that this is a serious project until we have some sort of confirmation.'

All the same, I toss and turn that night in bed. I feel the presence of the outside world closing in on what has been our domain. A cold breeze seems to move through the hut and a deep shiver touches my anxious body.

18

Outside Influences

Not long after Arnold's report, our second year on Caroline draws to an end. It's September and most of our stored food is finished. The time has come to pay our annual visit to the civilised world – first, to restock with a year's supply of bought food, and second, to haul out the boat and give it its coat of anti-fouling paint. Third, we'll visit the dentist and renew any out-of-date medical supplies. All in all, it should take no more than three weeks. We should be back on Caroline before the beginning of the cyclone season.

To avoid the chaos and stress of downtown Papeete, this year we sail directly to Moorea to do our shopping. We anchor in the relative quiet of Cook's Bay among the cruising yachts and a large visiting cruise ship.

Our first visit is to Captain Darr. He tells us, 'I know nothing about my lease except that it expires in October this year. The Kiribati government still hasn't replied to my letters.' He also says he knows nothing about a Mr Alex Orama, the French Polynesian businessman who is supposedly obtaining the new lease on Caroline Atoll that begins in November. We figure that the mysterious Mr Orama is likely to live or at least do business in Papeete, since that's the capital of French Polynesia. After taking the ferryboat to Papeete and making some inquiries, we track him down at the Café du Port, which we're told he owns, located not far from the seafront. The girl behind the bar contacts him by telephone. After a short conversation she informs us that he will come immediately.

I suppose all late-night bars look a little sordid in the fresh morning light. The Café du Port is no exception. Bare boards show through worn holes in the floor covering and white rips decorate the black plastic upholstery. Discoloured walls bear witness to the nightly smoky atmosphere. A well-used piano, guitar and ukulele rest abandoned in a corner for the day, ready to be picked up later for another night's festivities. The couple behind the bar wouldn't look inappropriate alongside Al Capone. We wait in silence, feeling totally out of place and alienated by this nightclub ambience. Our ragged sun-faded shirts, soiled cotton shorts and plastic sandals don't help.

Orama arrives without too much delay. His solid build is smartly dressed in a business suit and he carries a large square businessman's briefcase. I would describe him as middle aged. His skin is dark Polynesian, but somewhere in his background there is a mix of Asian or European blood. He orders a coffee and we accept his offer of an orange juice. As we settle opposite him across a small table, we are confronted by three heavy gold pendants that hang around his neck. Black coral, black pearls and jewels struggle for prominence against his white shirt. One wrist supports three gold bracelets, the other a large gold watch.

Anne is tense. Orama speaks no English, and my French is poor.

'Please just act as interpreter,' I warn her. 'Otherwise it could get very complicated.'

Orama tells us that once he was a bodyguard to the president of French Polynesia. Anne translates this into English before he continues. He explains how he was the first private investigator to have a practice in Tahiti. Now he owns this café, a hotel in the suburbs of Papeete and two old harbour tugs that he has converted into fishing boats.

He's surprised to learn that we have spent two years living on Caroline Atoll. He questions us about the number of turtles, lobsters, coconut crabs and fish. We explain about the difficulties of anchoring and the limitations of the pass. He tells us the pass is 'no problem'. He has a plan to dynamite a large new pass on the lee side of the island. Anne, unsettled by this information, begins to tell him that would be a mistake and a disaster for the lagoon.

I don't want any confrontation with Orama. I want information on his situation. I ask Anne again just to act as interpreter and stay cool. But I know what she's thinking. Because Caroline's lagoon is completely enclosed, when the tide is fully out, the water in the lagoon remains at least one foot above the low seawater level. Creating an outlet in the form of a pass would lower the whole level of the lagoon with the result that all the top coral would die, along with the thousands of Tridacna clams that live close to the surface. Broken coral would also encourage the algae that make the fish poisonous. This would be bad not only for us but also for his possible commercial fishing project.

Orama listens attentively to Anne's concern but appears totally unaffected. He continues to explain his future project. 'I'm going to build an airstrip,' he says, 'then a hotel with bungalows, a fishing industry, a turtle farm, a cultured pearl farm, a casino and a nudist colony. Why not?' he smiles, as Anne shakes her head in disbelief. 'I already have full local immigration clearance to ship Kiribati citizens through French Polynesia to work on Caroline as cheap labour,' he continues.

As if in response to our growing alarm and obvious lack of belief in his proposed schemes, Orama opens his briefcase.

Inside lies a brand new Kiribati national flag. He moves it aside to produce a letter from the Kiribati government. I'm surprised when he passes this letter over for me to read.

It's written in English. Although I'm a little embarrassed to be reading someone else's mail and don't want to linger too long over the details, I do read enough to establish that it is only a letter of guarantee that, after the government carries out a full land survey of the island, they will negotiate for a lease for fishing rights plus a piece of land for a shore base. I hand him back his proof of credibility. I wonder now – with his total lack of English – whether he fully realises the limitations and contents of this letter. It's certainly not the same kind of lease that Omer Darr had, which gave him total land rights and more or less a free hand to do as he pleased. Mr Orama goes on to assure us graciously that our presence on Caroline is in no way detrimental to his grandiose plans. For him at least there is no doubt in his mind that he is the new Lord of Caroline.

'The land belongs to god,' he states expansively. He gestures with his arms, spreading them wide open. There he rests for a moment, Christ-like on his own cross.

Outside the café, all Anne's pent-up anger explodes. 'Just imagine the disaster a dynamited pass would cause!' she repeats over and over. 'And a casino on Caroline, can you imagine?'

'According to his letter, Orama has a guarantee of fishing rights plus a piece of land – that's all,' I explain, 'and even that has to wait for a full land survey of the island.'

'And what about the airstrip and hotel and nudist colony?' she queries.

'He's dreaming, like we all do. It might be possible to build a Las Vegas on Caroline, but you're talking about a multimillion-dollar project with supply ships, international air service, full medical services – the whole show. Caroline is too fragile and isolated for such a large commercial development. Even if such a project could be realised, it would have to be financed by a very large enterprise, and not by a hotel and café owner with two old tugboats.'

'So, what do we do?' she asks anxiously.

'Under Omer's lease we're still legal until the end of October. If there are going to be boats and fishermen around the island, perhaps the Kiribati government would be interested in having an independent guardian on the island – namely, us.'

We stay in Moorea and do most of our shopping at the local supermarket. It costs us a little more but it is decidedly less stressful than downtown Papeete. But eventually we're obliged to visit Papeete for the boat haul-out and visit to the dentist. Anne updates all our medical supplies and does a final shop. Our most unusual purchase this year is a large roll of black plastic mesh for a new fish trap.

We have a pleasant surprise waiting for us in the mail. Carol, an old sailing friend who now lives in Fiji, has sent us a large, proper wheat grinder.

I quickly tire of thinking of ways to regularise our situation. I want to stay correct and legal but it's not looking possible. I long for the quiet sanity of Caroline, but I wonder how much longer we can resist being sucked into the spinning whirlpool that threatens to capture us in its vortex.

Arriving back at Caroline, we have the usual physical challenge of negotiating Blind Passage.

'We've always made it,' I say to Anne.

'It's bad,' she states.

'I know it's bad but we've always made it,' I repeat. One day this pass may be our ruin, but not today. Wildly we slither down that last wave to enter the gates of heaven safely once more.

After all the rich vegetation of the high volcanic islands

of Moorea and Tahiti, Ana-Ana looks dry and yellow. Nevertheless, the bananas, papayas, small trees and flowering bushes have all survived. Also this year I left two inverted twenty-litre containers of wheat with fine wire mesh over the opening so that the hens could only pick out the wheat grains one at a time. Although both containers are empty, the hens appear to be in good health and have remained around the house.

With the new wheat grinder I can hand-grind enough flour for the day in ten minutes. This is faster and less trouble than setting up the windmill on the beach. For the now redundant wind machine I have another idea.

I attach a long pole to the main wheel just a little off centre. As the wheel turns, this pole pumps up and down. The centre of this pole is fixed loosely to the frame with a stretching rope. A fishing buoy on the end now plunges into an open container of laundry, sweeps across the bottom, then rises up to continue its pumping and circular movement in the tub. The windmill becomes the wind-washing machine. It works. It's fun. However, the energy required to transport the water to fill the container, set up the sail wings and untwist the tangles in the laundry soon reaches the level of a chore. We revert to our usual habit of washing our few clothes and bedsheets by hand, close to the water supply. The wonderful wind-washer goes the way of the shower hoisting and smelly fish-sauce fertiliser – and not only because it's inconvenient.

On our isolated island, we realise, every decision needs to be evaluated as to whether we might be creating something that will get out of hand or spoil our interdependent environment. The windmill could have become a monster – its whipping blades could have injured the children or animals. When you're responsible for everything beyond what nature put there, you're constantly faced with making choices in the absence of rules. Of course, even rules don't always help in 'civilised' society. So often we do things just because they're possible, or to prove they're possible, without considering whether some of these innovations will cause more problems than they solve.

Not long after we arrive, Bill and Georgina, two coffee klatch friends who live on the island of Raiatea, give us a radio call. 'We've just met a friend of yours here, Ron,' Bill says in his usual loud manner. 'Bernard Moitessier – he says he's coming up to visit you.'

'That's very interesting, Bill. It's been two years since Bernard and Veronique last visited. Please say hello.'

'What do you think if I send you up some ducks?' he adds with a chuckle.

My first thought is for Bernard's crumb-free boat. 'That's all right by me if it's all right by Bernard. Don't ducks need fresh water?'

'No problem. They live here around the house without water, they breed fast and roast well and you'll love them. If you want I can send you up a goat as well.' He laughs over the airwaves. Anne is furiously shaking her head. I'm thinking, fresh goat's milk and cheese. Then I consider a captive goat on board *Tamata*. It would be too much. I agree with Anne that the ducks will be sufficient.

One week later the children alert us to an approaching yacht. 'It's Bernard, he's already in the pass!'

Soon we're all sitting comfortably in *Tamata*'s cockpit. Bernard has aged since his last visit, and Veronique confirms later that he is having problems with his health.

Between biscuits, the children fix their attention on the three bamboo boxes tied to *Tamata*'s back rail. Bernard shows them the ducks and explains that they are large Muscovy ducks. Bill has already named them 'Mr and Mrs Duck', along with their daughter, the 'Virgin Mary'. He has also sent up about two hundred books that have collected around his house over the years.

Once ashore, the ducks install themselves immediately and forever around the kitchen. They eat all the fish leftovers and snap at any flies or moths that come their way. In the evenings they terrorise the local cockroaches that so far have had this territory to themselves.

Bernard is passionately interested in everything we've done on the island since his last visit. He checks the saltiness of our well and examines the construction of the houses. He looks intently at the ferroconcrete tank and bottom-flashing barbecue. We show him the disused windwasher and the inactive solar shower. His attention finally focuses on the garden.

'Compost, Ron. What you really need here is good compost – you'll see it will make all the difference to your garden.' In principle I am the first to agree, but I mention that there's not enough organic material. Not at all disheartened, he goes on to explain: 'I knew an experienced gardener who lived in the Tuamotus who made compost using only the green leaves of the *Tournefortia* trees. When analysed, this compost was found to be complete.'

It's worth a try, I agree. Already I begin to feel my old reluctance about outside intrusions into my established and satisfyingly controlled routine. By agreeing, I am also obliged to cut into my new roll of plastic mesh to form a circular compost container four feet high by four feet in diameter.

Straightaway we begin to harvest the *Tournefortia* leaves from the lowest trees along the beach. Hour after hour we work under the blazing sun to fill our baskets. We carry our full baskets back to the settlement and tip them into the filling compost container. By the end of the day all the beach trees have been stripped clean. They stand there silhouetted and bare against the setting sun as if a swarm of locusts had just passed.

Next day when our visitors arrive, I'm busy enlarging the kitchen table to create a double bed so that they can sleep comfortably ashore under the kitchen roof. Bernard has other ideas about how to spend our time.

'Hen sheet, Ron. We must collect the hen sheet.'

'Yes,' I say, 'the hen's shit.'

The bed project is laid aside while we head for the hen house. Under the sloping night perches we support a large plastic sheet so that all the hen droppings will roll down to collect in a long trough along the bottom. The whole time we work, Bernard continues to assure me that 'hen sheet is so good.'

Next morning, his new surprise is the careful present-ation of a small metal container. 'Sheet, Ron. We have to collect all the human sheet and pees.' He ceremoniously hands over his morning's contribution. 'Sheet and pees are dynamite,' he insists.

I know he is probably right. What I'm thinking about now is losing our precious morning routine out on the reef. This simple and agreeable habit has developed into some-thing of a ritual. It's our community time as we crouch over the water, waiting for the sergeant majors. We talk about nothing in particular, with lots of jokes and laughter, and it has become one of the special moments of the day that I don't want to give up.

I'm not going to win, however. Popular opinion domin-ates and says that it's important that we collect all our shit and dynamite piss. I spend my morning constructing a toilet in the woods a little downwind from the house. I provide a comfortable seat and place a plastic bucket under the hole.

The frenzy of collecting is not finished. The next day Bernard decides that we should now systematically gather up all the numerous black sea slugs that lie in the shallows around Ana-Ana. This time I plead other priorities like baking the bread. Today the editor has no problem with his bread headlines: 'Shit', 'Piss' and 'Sea Slugs'.

As for the team, they spend their day wading around in the shallow water while I watch bucket after bucket of cleaned and sliced-up sea slugs arrive to be spread out over the now sizeable compost pile. I overhear Bernard explain in detail to his workers the best, fastest and most efficient way that he has so far developed to dissect and quarter the common sea slug.

Everything for the compost heap has to be carefully chopped up and spread out between layers of a mix of leaves and the black ground from Pig Islet. The human and hen 'sheet' is buried deep down and everything is damped down with the dynamite 'pees'. Finally, the local sharks go hungry as the overnight catch of rats is dropped one by one down small round holes that penetrate to the centre of the already warming pile. The mixed brew is then covered with old sacks.

The temperature in the tropics, ideal for wine and yoghurt making, is also perfect for the breaking down of compost. After only two days the compost is steaming hot and begins to give off a very distinctive sweet fermenting odour. Bernard predicts that in only one month the compost will be mature enough to add to the garden.

With the compost finally laid to rest, our visitors join us in our more normal island routine. I discover that Bernard plays the harmonica well. Eventually he tells me that he once performed on a local radio program when he lived in Vietnam. Using a double-sided Hohner, he has some fancy vamping techniques and a way to turn his harmonica over fast to find some half-notes that are missing on the other side's major scale. With some tense and nervous trial efforts, we succeed in harmonising a small program of popular standards.

It's time to face the workforce of bees again. This time I take Veronique along for moral support. For whatever reason, perhaps experience, perhaps a female presence, I'm altogether more cool and confident. Nevertheless, I take the extra precaution of wearing two pairs of socks and a shirt under my smock. Quietly and methodically, I pull out the full honeycombs, brush off the bees and replace the empty combs. The bees tolerate their familiar intruder, and I'm not stung once. Back at the house, with the willing help of two licky-sticky-fingered children, we supply *Tamata* with a large jar of coconut honey and add another five kilos to our supplies.

The next day Bernard complains about the taste of our water. I explain that we have a tiny parasite that comes from the trees and turns our water cloudy. He listens with interest to my explanation but thinks it's possibly something else. Anne also tastes the water and agrees that it's stronger than usual. More to humour the discontented than from any conviction, I take a look into the ten-litre plastic water container we've been using that sits on the kitchen shelf. I discover a very dead and bloated rat floating on the surface. Fortunately, no one becomes sick, and the semi-decomposed victim becomes a little plus for the semi-decomposed compost heap.

That night for entertainment I set up the rat cage on the kitchen shelf. We all watch the cage slowly fill up with rats – that is, all except one who repeatedly enters the cage but keeps his back feet solidly down on the trapdoor, then exits with each fresh piece of coconut.

'Look!' I laugh and say to Anne, 'my cousin.'

Our guests announce that their visit with us is coming to an end. Despite his health problems, Bernard has been

Bernard and has left his mark on Caroline. As they leave, I once more experience the sadness of parting, tinged with relief at the prospect of being left alone in peace.

PART THREE

Letting Go

19

A Forecast of Stormy Weather

The day our visitors leave, we begin work on the new fish trap. We use the same funnel of coral stones as before, but instead of the wire basket at the exit, we construct a large heart-shaped pen. With the heavy crowbar I make holes in the coral, hammer in Nono posts cut level to a little above the highest high water level, then add a top rail. We fold the plastic mesh over the frame and tie it to the posts and rail. Along the bottom we place large pieces of coral.

On our first attempt we round up a shoal of around fifty large parrotfish and chase them right into the trap. They swim around and around but fail to notice the open entrance located in the centre of the pen. Now we simply hand-spear enough fish for the day and leave the larder full for tomorrow.

We return the next day to the trap, anticipating a fresh harvest. But as we approach the small pass, it becomes evident that all is not well. The trap is filled with at least twenty large, black-tipped sharks. All the parrotfish have gone. We watch this mass of dorsal fins thrash to and fro as the sharks, panicked by our close presence, build into a desperate frenzy and begin to charge into the mesh.

'They're going to wreck the trap!' Anne cries. 'Kill them all and we'll have no more trouble.'

I don't want to kill them. I have nothing against sharks – they exist, for the most part, in balance with us. I give them respect, keep out of their way and have no war with them. Besides, the 'French Revolution' mentality may provide a temporary solution, but not a permanent one – there are always more sharks close at hand ready to take over.

'They're going to wreck the trap,' she warns again.

I pick up my heavy spear. Still I hesitate, a little fascinated by all the action so close at hand. Then one five-foot-long shark punches a hole right through my precious mesh. I attack. Other sharks begin to break through the mesh. It's a war zone – and a massacre ensues. Some sharks escape, but most lie dead or dying on the dry reef. The trap is a mess of broken mesh. It takes hours of patience to repair all the damage.

Before we leave, I hammer in a row of narrowly spaced steel bars right across the entrance. 'To keep the sharks out and let the fish in,' Alexandre explains to his ever-questioning sister. This modification works well. From then on, no more sharks enter the trap.

We sail back across the lagoon with the taste of violence in our mouths and fifteen bloody sharks at our feet.

'Come and see this,' Anne beckons as she cuts up the sharks for the newest compost pile. In each shark's stomach she discovers half a dozen large parrotfish, as neatly packed as sardines in a tin.

Later that same day I notice that one of our two parakeets, Kwili, is quieter than usual. 'So, what's wrong with you?' I ask with my nose against the cage.

He gives me one last long look, then just topples over in front of my eyes. By the time I reach into his cage, he's quite dead. Death has had a busy day!

'We'll make him a grave like they did for the baby,'

Alexandre says as the loss of one of our crew is fully absorbed.

'With a coral stone,' Anaïs adds to try to help.

Together we choose a suitable place within sight of the house and under the shade of a young Nono tree. There we dig Kwili's last resting place. A small headstone of flat coral still marks his peaceful spot.

Raki, Kwili's companion, now looks a little sad and lonely. After some discussion we decide to leave his cage door open so that he can choose his freedom. At first afraid, eventually he moves to the outside of his protective prison. For a few days he stays around the house, apparently confused about how to handle his new-found liberty. One day he just flies away.

We look for him on South Islet, guessing that he may have headed for the relatively large forest and land mass there. We call Raki over and over again but he is not to be found. I like to imagine him still very alive and involved, as Dou-Dou was before him, in a grand if futile search for a loving mate.

Mrs Duck, on the other hand, has maintained a seemingly satisfying and regular sex life – mostly in front of the kitchen table. She has produced a grand total of eighteen large eggs. Now she is brooding on a coral nest under the house, faithfully bringing her pleasures and production into being.

The sex life of the Virgin Mary, although active, is not quite as uncomplicated. A young cock has fallen desperately in love with her and, much to her confusion and the annoyance of Mr Duck, mounts her two or three times each day.

The ducks, unlike the chickens, seem socially connected to each other. When one gets his leg caught in a plastic bag, the others surround him, offering comments on what to do. When I play music, they all settle down in front of me as a group, like a human audience. Unlike our species, however, they display no anxiety about the future, no prejudice, no deviousness. Although some have good memories, they are not burdened by huge piles of information or dogma. They do display emotion but their heads stay clear. Their simple way of relating, I think, provides a good example to follow.

Back in the garden I uncover the compost pile. All that remains from the breakdown of Bernard's exotic ingredients is a solid black and healthy-looking soil. Systematically I add this recreated food to all the plants around the garden. Within days the effects are evident and in some cases incredible. Our already quite respectable banana trees begin to put out oversized dark green leaves that give the impression of giants' arms reaching toward the sky. Gradually, as the wonder food is fully absorbed by all the plants, our garden transforms before our eyes into a place of otherworldly lushness.

'Dynamite,' Anne says with appropriate reverence for Bernard, her self-sufficiency guru.

'Dynamite,' I agree.

One day in February, our normal sunny sky turns cloudy and the weather begins to deteriorate. I contact Arnold in search of consolation. 'What's happening, Arnold? It's blowing half a gale here and raining like the second flood's coming.'

'What you have is a tropical depression forming very close to you. There's also another depression six hundred miles to your west. If they join up and intensify, which is very possible, you could have a cyclone right on your doorstep.'

'Okay, Arnold – always bad news from you. Thanks for the warning.'

The wind increases, and the house shakes with each fresh gust that finds its way over the trees into the clearing. Our large hanging shutters lift up with each puff, then crash back down against their frames. The rain is continuous and heavy.

First I tie down the shutters, then run ropes right over the roof and fix them to the base of the nearby trees. The atmosphere inside the closed house is dark and depressing. The children take their games outside and under the house where there is more light and air.

'The little ducks are coming,' Anaïs sings out from deep in their refuge.

'Ducks like rain,' I tell her, 'but they could have picked a better time.'

'There are two and they're yellow,' she cries out. 'They're looking at me.'

The wind builds up to a steady forty knots with gusts of over fifty knots that lift spray from the mass of 'white horses' which now race each other across the surface of the lagoon. The rain is being blown almost horizontal. For a moment the terrible weather and sad, grey atmosphere bring on a wave of nostalgia for my old home in always-rainy Scotland. Visibility falls to around two hundred yards. From time to time I catch a glimpse of *Fleur d'Ecosse* heeled hard over and straining at her moorings. In these circumstances, there is no way I can cross the lagoon to check her mooring ropes.

My small rain-measuring butter tin, normally adequate for our typical prolonged tropical showers, has overflowed after measuring its maximum of three inches in the last few hours. A larger and taller milk tin replaces it.

The hens remain in the relative safety of their hen house, huddling close together on their perches for warmth and comfort. Only Mr Duck and the Virgin Mary appear completely unaffected by the worsening conditions. Calm and contented, they use the downpour as an opportunity to clean and preen their feathers.

'There are two more babies,' Anaïs continues to report, peeking out from under the house like a little duck herself.

The wind becomes stronger. Branches begin to break off and crash to the ground. On the beach our landing is packed with a solid mass of debris and branches swept from across the lagoon. Large swells from the centre of the storm start to flood up and over the reef. These enormous masses of solid water run on between the islets like a tidal bore in an estuary. A new bore around three feet high runs through every few minutes to empty into the lagoon. Already the lagoon, two feet higher than normal, covers all our lowest land area. A deep fresh-water lake has formed around the low basin where I dug the well.

Night comes and the storm continues. The children, with Kiki and Dou-Dou close beside them, sleep on through the terrible noise of the wind howling in the trees and branches breaking.

'It's getting worse,' Anne says as another gust rocks the house in the darkness.

Before I can reply, a solid thump makes both of us sit upright on the bed. Outside, aided by the flashlight, we search through the pitch darkness.

'There!' Anne says. We're looking at our best heavy-laden papaya tree, which lies flat at our feet, having being snapped clean in two. A banana plant close by has suffered the same plight.

Back in bed, we listen nervously in the eerie darkness to the rising sounds of rushing water as the now gigantic swells surge across the reef. The gurgle of agitated water is frighteningly close as the growing swells force water farther and farther up the banks of Ana-Ana.

'I'm going to empty the tank,' I say quietly.

'Yes,' Anne agrees with equal calm. 'I'll pack the tins.'

As our priorities change, I have little concern for our

months and months of carefully collected drinking water. Quickly I open the tap and uncork the bottom drain of the tank. A new flood now starts as 2500 litres of water cut a deep groove down past the kitchen to join the new lake by the well. In one hour the tank is empty.

I climb inside the tank. The noise of the storm ceases to exist. The sounds of my movements echo from the walls as I dry up the small pools that remain on the floor. Anne manages a smile when she passes in a plastic container with twenty litres of water. She has been busy and continues to hand down large biscuit boxes filled with emergency food, clothes, matches, flashlight, hooks and nylon.

'Don't forget a machete,' I remind her as I arrange the boxes.

Finally, the transceiver radio arrives, and I take a break. It's late and I'm tired.

The tank now prepared for the worst, I can relax a little. While Anne searches around for anything she may have forgotten, I remain inside the tank. I smile to myself as I sit quietly remembering Anaïs's true prediction that there is not going to be much room in the tank. My eyes close as my thoughts drift to imagine the worst possible situation where Ana-Ana becomes completely flooded and the tank could become buoyant and float away.

Bump, scrape, bump – the tank moves.

'We're floating,' I say and check that the top cover is tightly sealed. We're pushed around but remain fairly comfortable bobbing slowly up and down like a navigation buoy.

'We're all right,' I say over and over again. 'We're all right. We have enough food and water and the radio.' When we feel the seas calm down, I open the top cover to a bright shining sun.

'You see, we've survived!' I exult, then become totally

absorbed in the practical problem of raising the radio antenna.

'Woohoo!' I hear through my absorption from far away. I wake up to find Anne looking down through the hatch with the last box of medical supplies. I blink up at her in surprise.

'You were sleeping,' she says. A spasm of relief passes through my body as I realise I am still sitting on the hard dry ground of Ana-Ana. I mumble, 'Yes, I guess I was.'

The rest of the night we spend in the house while the conditions outside remain bad but do not deteriorate. The morning light reveals the damage of the night. Broken trees and branches cover the coral around the house. Many more of our papaya and banana plants have their heads lying low to the ground. I'm relieved to catch a glimpse of *Fleur d'Ecosse* still firmly on her mooring. As the day develops and brightens, the conditions continue to improve.

'You were pretty lucky, Ron,' Arnold informs us on the evening net. 'Your depression moved away to join the other depression centred over the Northern Cook Islands. It's now a full-blown cyclone, which has been named "Penny". It has winds over one hundred knots per hour. It's heading south.'

The next day the sun is shining and the easterly trade wind returns. The hens come out from the shelter of their hen house, ruffle their feathers and go on an immediate search for food. Mrs Duck emerges with twelve ducklings. We watch amazed as the day-old ducklings lead their mother directly to the flooded fresh-water lake at the bottom of the garden. There they delight in an early morning swim. The rainfall over the last three days measures out at nineteen inches.

That night, Radio Tahiti announces that Cyclone Penny has reached the Society Islands and caused widespread devastation to houses and property on the island of Bora-Bora.

We have survived Penny. In the aftermath of our big storm, I wonder how we will handle the other source of depression building up over our horizon: Mr Orama's dreams of dynamite, tugboats and hotels.

20

Of Scientists and Fishermen

One month has gone by since the passing of Penny. Ana-Ana is beginning to look respectable again, and our lives have returned to a more normal routine. Then one day the children come rushing back to the house shouting, 'A yacht! A yacht in the pass! But whose is it?'

'It must be *Te Manu*, "the Bird" in Tahitian,' I tell them.

Graham Wragg, the captain of what he describes as a scientific survey vessel, has already checked into the radio net to tell us he will be arriving with a survey team.

'We have Kay Kepler aboard,' he explained. 'She was on Caroline once before as part of a Russian-American expedition aboard the Russian ship *Akademik Korolev*. Now she's part of an international survey team who want to survey other isolated islands belonging to the Republic of Kiribati. Right now we want to spend a few days on Caroline.'

We have just begun to prepare for these visitors when the children cry out again, 'A boat! A big boat on the other side of the island. Come and see, come and see!'

This time it's a tugboat about sixty feet long and can only be one of Mr Alex Orama's fishing boats. I wonder what turn of fate has brought these two boats to Caroline at exactly the same moment, with such totally opposed

interests. The biologists are here to investigate the uniquely
pristine state of Caroline's environment, which they want
to keep that way. Orama is interested only in the complete
exploitation and rape of the atoll.

Between gathering the blossoms of the *Cordia* tree and
threading their necklaces, the children excitedly keep us
informed on the two ships. *Te Manu* has a rubber dinghy in
the water with a motor on the back. Orama's tugboat,
Saturne, can't find a place to anchor, so he has an aluminium
boat in the water and a big motor.

I rake over the paths, sweep out the house and put things
in their place. Anne clears the breakfast table and brings in
more benches.

'The rubber dinghy is coming across the lagoon,' our
lookouts cry. 'It's full of people. They're almost here.' *Saturne*
is forgotten for a moment as we head to the beach to
welcome the biologists.

A tall, fresh-looking young man steps out first from the
dinghy. 'Ron, I'm Graham. How do you do?' Five other
people step ashore, and we exchange handshakes all round.
The children hold on to their floral necklaces. They have
a problem: they don't have enough for everyone.

'This is Kay,' Graham says as he introduces the eldest
member of the group. 'Anne, Mark and John are also biologists and come from England,' he continues. 'Alve is
Swedish and my first mate aboard.'

We all agree that Kay and Captain Graham qualify for
the necklaces. The large group of people has made Anaïs a
little shy. To comfort her I lift her up so she can place the
necklaces around their necks.

'Well, welcome to Ana-Ana,' I say as we head through
the trees. The group follows, enclosed in a babble of conversation – a sound strange to the island.

We're just arriving at the house when a small group of

Tahitians appears through the trees. We all meet up at the front of the house at exactly the same time. I wonder again at the ironic timing of fate. The captain of *Saturne* introduces himself and his first mate. The rest of the rough-looking crew of six hold back and disperse around the house. They are all stripped to the waist and wear head-bands like pirates.

The air is filled to absorption with cross conversations in French, English and Tahitian. One Tahitian crew member demands a machete. I hesitate about handing over a possible weapon. Sensitive to my anxiety, he quickly assures me that he only wants to open coconuts.

The crew brings bunches of green coconuts to the house. They strip off the outer husks, then cut out neat round drinking-holes on top. They make a kind of ceremony out of the presentation of one coconut for each person, with jokes and funny gestures, so that any feelings of conflict disappear in the simplicity of human interaction. The atmosphere becomes light and amusing.

In the short space of one hour Ana-Ana's population has risen from four to eighteen people. By mutual agreement we decide to share the midday meal. The Tahitians bring in fresh fish from their boat plus packets of rice and some defrosted French baguettes. The biologists contribute tins from their expedition rations. Anne and Alve cut out and prepare the heart-of-palm salad. I collect tomatoes, long green beans and some papayas from the garden. It's an extraordinary gathering. The fish is grilled; coconuts are grated and squeezed for their milk; leaves are produced for plates. We eat with our fingers.

Anne becomes excited and animated by all this unusual company. Alexandre attaches himself to Graham and follows him around watching everything he does. Anaïs follows Alexandre. I take a moment to wonder how this mixed group would evolve if we were all marooned here. One problem is immediately apparent: we adults are thirteen males to three females.

The settling of Pitcairn Island (not too far from here) by the mutineers of the *Bounty* and the Polynesians who accompanied them was a bloody affair. Apart from obvious cultural and character clashes, there were too many single males, and conflict erupted over the women. This fundamental problem had terrible repercussions and led to violence and murder until eventually most of the males were killed.

After the meal and at the insistence of the happy-go-lucky Tahitians, I bring out Anne's guitar. I take the opportunity also to try out my new combination of autoharp and harmonica. We play together and a singsong begins that continues all afternoon. The program is as varied as our international group with Tahitian, American, Scottish, English, French and Swedish songs all being well represented.

Finally all the pots are washed and put away and everything is tidied up before our guests depart for their respective boats. An air of quiet and peace – that for once feels quite strange – descends on Ana-Ana.

When the biologists arrive early the next morning, they are rested and eager to start work. They have all decided that they prefer to sleep ashore rather than return each evening to the cramped quarters of the boat. They have brought with them thin camping mattresses and a few private belongings.

Kay Kepler joins us at our breakfast table. She explains a little about her work and her particular interest in Caroline. From the survey she completed with her husband at the time of the Russian ship, she has produced two thick volumes with details about Caroline's environment. Every last small islet has been named and drawn out in detail. All the various trees and bushes have been listed and shown in their appropriate positions. Each islet is accompanied by a full list of the number and type of birds, rats, lizards, land crabs and coconut crabs that live there, plus any other unusual features. The details are long and impressive. I read one summary page:

Caroline Atoll has 39 islets, 26 types of plants and 15 bird species.

The birds:

Migrating Sooty Terns	900,000
Black Noddies	17,000
Brown Noddies	3,000
Blue-Gray Noddies	10
White Terns	8,000
Red Footed Boobies	7,000
Masked Boobies	400
Brown Boobies	40
Great Frigate Birds	6,088
Lesser Frigate Birds	200
Red Tailed Tropic Birds	150
Reef Herons	50
Lesser Golden Plovers	30
Ruddy Turnstones	5
Long Tailed Cuckoo	4

The details go on and on. It's another view of Caroline, seen through the eyes of an analyst. Kay is passionate and enthusiastic about her work and the island. 'Caroline is one of the most beautiful and pristine islands in the whole Pacific, or possibly in the whole world,' she says. 'It's a rare gem. It's also vulnerable. Along with its one million seabirds, it needs protecting.' She is totally opposed to Orama's proposed activities and fears for the exploitation of the green turtle, coconut crab, seabirds, lobsters, marine crabs and fish. She tells us that she's working with an international conservation agency to declare and manage Caroline as a World Heritage Site or Nature Conservancy Preserve. She says that, with the help of this international agency, she has made an appeal to the Kiribati government to keep Caroline's treasure intact and to stop the commercial exploitation by Orama.

'How would you like to be the guardian for the Conservation Agency?' she asks.

'Kay, can you think of anything better than to be the guardian of your own dream?' I reply sincerely. But at the same time, I foresee the potential build-up of a grand conflict of dreams and schemes between Kay Kepler and Alex Orama, with us caught somewhere in the middle, the victims of a conflict which is not ours. This is not a comfortable thought. Indeed, my innocent agreement to act as guardian will have nasty repercussions, as it turns out.

Conservation is a fine ideal and absolutely necessary if we are to preserve nature's diminishing presence on our planet. In the meantime the expanding human population is also struggling to survive. In particular, the new Republic of Kiribati is a poor country with enormous problems of administration and transport over its widely scattered islands. I know they are more interested in commercial projects, which help to combat their day-to-day problems, than in ideals. In the Pacific islands, where fish and wildlife are still abundant, the need to protect nature is not as obvious as it is in more developed countries.

I explain all this to Kay and tell her I think she may have problems. 'Plus,' I add, 'Orama is not against us remaining here, in principle. Even if we support your goals one hundred per cent, it would be against our own interests to be part of any open confrontation.'

Graham arrives and our discussion is cut short. He is ready to transport all the biologists on an expedition up the lagoon. Kay is particularly interested in comparing any differences in the islets since the passing of Cyclone Penny.

No sooner have the biologists left than the Tahitians arrive, keen to find the best place in the lagoon for a large fish trap. I leave them to Anne and hear her insisting that there are no fish in any great numbers in the lagoon itself. 'Yes, maybe in the pass,' she concedes with some annoyance. 'Why don't you just go and look for yourselves?' Later on she is really fuming. 'Look at that!' she cries as the Tahitians' speedboat passes out over the reef, piled high with what I would estimate to be around one hundred glass and plastic buoys. 'They're taking all the fishing buoys.'

'We've taken a good share ourselves,' I try to console her. 'At least they are fishermen.'

'They've started,' she insists. 'They're not going to use them. They'll sell them in Papeete. It's all finished here. They're going to help themselves to everything and anything they can from this island.'

After the evening meal the biologists organise their sleeping quarters. Alve and Mark are to sleep on the bench-tables in the cookhouse. Kay, Anne, Graham and John are to sleep in the house. I'm surprised and impressed by the biologists' seriousness and dedication. They appear to be oblivious to any sense of their own personal comfort while they crawl through the jungle, are bitten by mosquitoes, are baked by the overhead sun, eat tasteless dry biscuits with cold food from tin cans and sleep on thin hard mattresses. All this, simply in order to count the number of birds and plants on an isolated island. I listen for hours to their discussions about the minor differences between the lesser and greater frigate bird.

In the morning the Tahitians arrive to say goodbye. They

have decided that the pass is the place for their fish trap and they tell us they have had some success trawling outside the reef for black jacks. They thank us for our hospitality, offer to take our mail and ask if we need any provisions that they could bring back. I hadn't thought of them as a possible mail service or source of food supply. I'm too surprised to take advantage of their offer.

'Next time,' I reply, 'we'll have a list ready.'

'No problems,' they say. 'In two weeks we will be back with materials for the trap.' After polite handshakes all round they leave.

The biologists remain around the house. Graham, always curious, has brought in his newest Magellan hand-held satellite navigation aid. 'Did you know that Caroline Atoll is actually half a mile east of its charted position?' he asks as he switches on this minicomputer. 'Look, if you check out the position of Ana-Ana on your chart, you will find that the GPS read-out puts us more than half a mile to the east. Arundel's chart of one hundred years ago has never been resurveyed. He hit upon the more or less correct latitude. But during this period it was difficult to arrive at an accurate time, so he slipped up a little with his longitude.'

'I wonder if I can remember enough about drafting to make a new chart?' I say more to myself as a question than as a suggestion.

'You'd be doing the British Admiralty and other navigators a favour if you could,' Graham says. 'If you want, I'll run you up the lagoon and we'll take GPS positions at various points around the atoll. Then, you can plot them out later and reposition the whole island.'

Kay, who is also enthusiastic about the possibility of an updated chart, leaves me a copy of a series of recent aerial photographs taken by a New Zealand survey plane. The black and white images clearly show the outer reef, lagoon and individual islets.

'These GPS fixes are accurate to within a few yards,' Graham assures me on our navigational survey trip. As we move about I methodically note down all his positional read-outs plus the computed distances between each point.

Alexandre and Anaïs have begun to adopt Graham as an uncle, which is quite strange as he tells us that his mother's family name is also Falconer and that her great-grandfather emigrated from Scotland over one hundred years ago.

'I may well be some sort of distant cousin,' he says thoughtfully.

Before leaving, Kay confides to us that, despite numerous applications to the Kiribati government, her team has in fact received no permission for this present survey. 'We're hoping to sort it out when we arrive at Christmas Island,' she says. 'Then, we'll see you again on our way back.' I'm forced to question her confidence about being able to create a World Heritage Site with the cooperation of a government that refuses to communicate.

Te Manu leaves and our routine becomes a little more normal. Then, exactly one month after leaving Caroline, *Saturne* is back.

'We're going to build a fish trap right across the pass,' declares the new foreman, Adrien, who is married to Orama's daughter.

'And my boat?' I ask. 'How am I going to get in and out?'

'Ah! Good point,' someone adds and we all laugh.

After much discussion and various suggestions, they agree to leave me a clear space along one side of the trap so that I can enter and leave without difficulty. Just to be sure of the arrangements I accompany them out to the pass.

They work hard and fast. They hammer one-inch bars deep into the virgin forest of live coral that runs up the pass, to form a large circle. Then they tie on vertically a full fifty-yard roll of six-foot-high galvanised mesh. In the same manner they form a funnelled entrance into their wired enclosure.

Their first victim is our green turtle, who has probably lived here in this pass peacefully and without interference for more than fifty years. Then our big quiet Napoleon fish slides inside before he realises he is trapped. I'm greatly upset. The turtle and the Napoleon were part of our extended family who we were always pleased to see each time we returned to the island. I've had enough and can watch no more. I leave the professionals to their work and return to Ana-Ana with the feeling that the precious gem of the Pacific has already begun to lose some of its sparkle.

'It's against the law to kill the turtles,' Anne storms.

'It's not unusual for Tahitians to eat turtles,' I remind her.

'They're not going to eat them!' she insists. 'They're going to sell them on the black market in Tahiti. I know some fishermen who actually pay for their boats by hunting turtles on the isolated islands.'

'They're building a hut on Puti-Puti,' she continues in her mood of indignation. 'It's facing Ana-Ana where the Russians had their camp.'

Next morning I wander over to the Tahitian encampment. Their hut is made from old rusty corrugated iron. They also have a dog. They welcome me in their usual friendly manner and pull in a log so that I can sit down in reasonable comfort. One Tahitian passes over a freshly opened green coconut.

'It's good here,' they say. 'Papeete, no good – too much noise, too many cars.'

I notice that I'm surrounded by a large group of coconut crabs that rest in frozen postures like statues in the Louvre. They have all been stopped in time as the result of being injected with formalin. 'To preserve them,' they explain, 'for the tourists.'

Later Anne reports that she saw another boatload of fishing buoys go out to *Saturne*.

After three days the Tahitians come by to say that they're leaving.

'So soon?' I question.

'We have to leave,' they explain. 'Our ice is melting.'

It appears they have no refrigeration on board and carry only iceboxes to preserve their catch. They also have another problem. The local sharks have picked up on their trolling system and now follow their speedboat to attack each fish as it's hooked and being pulled in. Only the head remains for the fishermen.

'Too bad,' they say. 'We've only half-filled our iceboxes.'

Then we learn that four of the Tahitians plan to stay on the atoll. 'To look after the fish trap,' they explain.

'We will be back in two weeks to collect all the fish they catch,' the captain states with confidence as *Saturne* leaves. This time they take our shopping list with them.

After *Saturne*'s departure, the new resident Tahitians stay busy around their camp for a few days. They build a second, smaller fish trap close to Puti-Puti. We accept their presence, as we've learned to accept most things about our lives here, but nevertheless question the changing status of the island and our isolation. Anne, not entirely comfortable with the thought of four healthy young males on the island, does not provoke them with her nudity.

Soon they begin to bring us fish and hang around the house. They are fed up, they say, and suggest we all eat together. They are pleasant company. We talk about Papeete, their families and their work. We play a little music together, and they are pleased to amuse Alexandre and Anaïs. After a few meetings we become familiar with their individual characters.

Adrien, by virtue of being married to Lena, Orama's daughter, is in charge. He is also the owner of the Alsatian dog, Rocky. He tells us he has just been released from prison after spending a year there for his part in riots which ended with the burning down of large sections of central Papeete. He was brought up in the town and is a motorbike enthusiast. He is physically well built, a little overbearing and not altogether comfortable with the coral atoll environment.

Jacob, who comes originally from the Tuamotus, is the most serious of the group. He is strong and confident in himself, and an excellent diver. He's a great guitar player and sings well too.

Marere tells us quite simply that he drinks too much in Papeete and sleeps in the streets. 'He's a tramp!' the others laugh. He's sensitive and nervous, and although serious and capable, mostly ends up acting the clown.

Gerald is the round, good-humoured cook. The others joke continually about his size and shape. He works hard and is uncomplaining.

They are all very polite and respectful with Anne. Rocky, their Alsatian dog, has no such reservations with Kiki who, on account of having lived an isolated and protected life on the boat and desert islands, is still a virgin. Plus, with her short legs and low-slung body, she presents a considerable handicap for long-legged Rocky. Passion, for better or for worse, has its way, and despite the physical difficulties, they both appear content with the end result of their copulation.

After seven days of Caroline's calm, the Tahitians have had enough peace and tranquillity and wait impatiently for the return of *Saturne*.

'*Saturne* has left for Caroline,' reports Jean, a radio operator who works in Papeete port, teaching navigation to future captains. He has recently joined the coffee klatch. It's been nine days since *Saturne* left Caroline, and our guests, delighted with the news, prepare their things to leave.

Saturne's voyage should take just a little over two days. When three days pass, the Tahitians begin to worry and spend all their time sitting far out on the reef. In solidarity they remain together, a small lonely group, staring hour after hour at the horizon, waiting for the tugboat to appear.

After five days Jean tells us that *Saturne* has in fact returned to Papeete. 'They couldn't find the atoll,' he explains. 'They have a new captain on board who doesn't fully understand the satellite navigation system, so they tried to find the island by following the compass course. I checked their compass and found a thirty-degree deviation error.'

Our Tahitians are depressed. We feel sorry for them, so as a distraction we invite them to the special dinner where we celebrate our first roast duckling. But despite our efforts, the non-arrival of their boat and transport has affected them deeply. Their adventure has started badly. I'm wondering, probably even more than they are, how it's going to continue.

21

New Invaders

The day after the news of *Saturne*, we have another surprise: a huge cruise ship slides down the lee side of the island and comes to a stop close behind Ana-Ana. I can read *WORLD DISCOVERER* painted boldly on her bow. Straightaway the crew members launch huge black inflatable Zodiacs and approach the reef like a marine assault team. The Tahitians, with little else to do, are quickly out on the reef to help the crew drag the large Zodiacs across the shallows of the reef into the lagoon. The tourists, meanwhile, sit contentedly inside the inflatables without getting their feet wet.

The visitors are then, of course, led directly around to Ana-Ana. Four Zodiacs, with twelve people in each boat, spill out onto our little beach. They follow our path through the trees and finally totally surround the house.

'This is ridiculous!' Anne fumes as she holds on tightly to Alexandre and Anaïs.

Cameras flash, and we're encircled by a large group of people who keep up a steady flow of questions: 'What do you do for water? What about medical help? Do you educate the children? Do you have cyclones? How long have you been here? How long are you going to stay? Were the children born here? Aren't you lonely?'

My attention is split between giving sensible answers and trying to keep an eye on what all these possible souvenir hunters are up to around the house. Then the questions suddenly stop, the group parts and I'm confronted by a large impressive-looking gentleman with a high forehead who simply stands there until he has my full attention.

'Bengt Danielsson!' he announces. Then he adds, 'Marie Therese!' and nods toward a small pleasant-looking lady by his side.

'Ron Falconer!' I respond with equal formality. Anne and the children have moved away, so I can't imitate the nodding gesture to introduce my family.

I'm quite familiar with the name of this imposing character before me. Bengt Danielsson was one of the members of Thor Heyerdahl's Kon-Tiki raft expedition. When the raft crash-landed on Raroia Atoll in the Tuamotus after its epic crossing of the Pacific Ocean, Danielsson remained on the atoll for an additional two years studying the lifestyle of the Polynesians. I also remember reading one of his many books on Polynesia called *Love in the South Seas*. He now lives in Tahiti.

'I'm lecturing on the *World Discoverer*,' he continues. 'Did you know that Caroline Atoll was discovered by Europeans long before Tahiti, Hawaii or the Cook Islands, simply because the earliest Pacific navigators chose to sail along the latitude of ten degrees south? It was the Portuguese explorer Pedro Fernando de Quirós who discovered Caroline as early as 1606. But it was Captain W. R. Broughton of the British sloop *Providence* who named the atoll "Caroline" in 1795 as a compliment to the daughter of Sir Stephens, the First Lord of the British Admiralty.'

He's a good lecturer, if a bit formal, but as I already know most of his information, my mind wanders. First the biologists, then Orama, and now *World Discoverer*. I imagine that if this trend continues, we could well be voted 'Atoll of the Year' by *Time* magazine with my new chart of Caroline on the front cover.

I give our distinguished guest a personal guided tour of the premises. We pose together on the steps of the house like movie stars while the cameras flash and the video cameras turn. Eventually, they all leave. Anne accompanies the group away from the house to act as guide for a tour up the lagoon to Nake Islet. Before she leaves, I tell her we've been invited out to the ship for lunch as the guests of Mr and Mrs Danielsson. With a quick raising of the eyebrows she indicates her acceptance of our new status as celebrities.

The Tahitians have also been invited out to the ship. They are pleased, their situation having suddenly changed from that of abandoned castaways to guests on one of the world's leading cruise ships. Their immediate problem is: what to wear? After a few minutes' discussion they discard their dirty, tattered T-shirts. Then, posing as bare-chested natives, they wear only their most respectable pair of shorts. As I watch them mixing with the guests, I'm surprised to see one of them hand over a large bunch of long red feathers. I realise they must have systematically stripped every last tail feather from the small colony of nesting red-tailed tropic birds near Nake Islet.

No one objects when I explain that Kiki also has to come aboard since, if she is left behind, she will attempt to swim out to sea, following us to the ship. Aboard the ship we are immediately taken into the style and comfort of the ship's luxury dining room. We sit nervously in our soiled clothes and coconut hats, a little awed by the atmosphere and stylish surroundings. Kiki lies quietly at our feet, enjoying the comfort of a thick carpet.

Alexandre and Anaïs are not so inhibited. They immediately begin to climb all over the smartly upholstered seats.

They are delighted when they discover that, if they stand on the varnished windowsills, they can see over the tops of Ana-Ana's trees into the lagoon. When they begin to play hide-and-seek in the thick plush velvet curtains, a uniformed stewardess appears and distracts them with presents before escorting them to a place far in the bowels of the ship.

We don't see them again for over an hour. No doubt, wide-eyed about all they see, they make good guests, easily entertained by the young hostesses. Finally, they arrive back with new T-shirts, some plastic toys and sweets from the ship's shop. They let us know they have also visited the top deck, swimming pool and games room.

Bengt Danielsson and Marie Therese join us at the table along with two other lecturers. We eat while listening to more historic and intellectual information about the Pacific islands and her peoples until Bengt Danielsson excuses himself and retires to his cabin. We then learn from Marie Therese that she is actively working to put an end to atomic testing in the Pacific and regularly attends international conferences all over the world.

Eventually, we're left alone with the quiet-spoken Edmundo, an archaeologist who lives on Easter Island. Charming and calm, he asks if there is anything we need from the ship's supplies. I can think of nothing special except perhaps a piece of steak or an apple. He returns after a short absence not only with a food package of the best steak and apples, but also with a hold-all full of wonderful books that have been left behind by the classy tourists that the *World Discoverer* caters for. How many times over the following months will I have cause to bless Edmundo, as each book that I pull out of the bag turns out to be a better-than-average read, with some very memorable ones too.

The Tahitians have their own adventure. They consume

a fair amount of beer, party with the guests and flirt with the stewardesses. By late afternoon it's all over. We stand together out on the reef waving goodbye, our heads still spinning from the whirlwind visit of the great *World Discoverer* to tiny Caroline Atoll.

'I had a very good day,' Alexandre announces as we prepare for bed.

'Me too,' Anaïs agrees, arranging all her gifts alongside her mattress.

'I feel like I've spent a day at the zoo,' is my contribution to the summing-up.

'Yes,' Anne agrees, 'only we were the animals!'

Another week passes before Jean informs us that *Saturne* has left Tahiti once again. But after three more days she still does not appear. The Tahitians again take up their vigil of sitting hour after hour out on the reef, looking towards the southern horizon.

'Come and listen to this!' I shout to Anne as I follow today's early-morning coffee klatch meeting.

'It looked like a tug,' the operator is saying. 'They motored straight for us and wanted to come aboard. Well, I refused, thinking they could be pirates. They spoke only a little English, but from what I could understand, they wanted to know their position and a compass course to Caroline Atoll.'

'It's *Saturne*,' I say excitedly to Anne. 'They're lost again.'

'We were pretty afraid,' the operator continues. 'They were a rough-looking crew. I stayed half hidden in the cockpit with a loaded rifle in my hand. Eventually, we gave them our position and a compass course direct for Caroline Atoll.'

I break into the conversation to ask the yacht what its position was when they met the tug.

'Wait a minute. I have it marked down,' the operator

says. 'We were almost one hundred miles due east of Caroline Atoll.'

'One hundred miles off course seems hardly possible,' Anne says. 'Can it really be *Saturne*?'

'It must be,' I insist. 'They should be here by now. Their navigation is all wrong and they're lost again.'

Three days later Jean confirms that *Saturne* is back in Papeete harbour.

'So, how do they find their way back each time?' Anne asks, still having difficulty accepting that an ocean-going tug could have such serious navigational problems.

'I suppose they just head south till they run into the long Tuamotu group of islands, then island-hop home from there. Plus, you can pick up the mountains of Tahiti from eighty miles away.'

The Tahitians are clearly distressed by this new information. I offer to try to set up radio contact with their families in Papeete. With the aid of Jean and a radio-telephone link-up, we connect Adrien directly to his wife. Lena explains that, indeed, they have had some problems, but they are now going to change the captain and try again. The radio-telephone link-up turns into a family reunion with Jacob, Marere and Gerald all taking turns on the microphone. They laugh and giggle and make continuous amorous suggestions to whoever is on the other end of the line.

As another week passes, the Tahitians call by each day for news.

'They tried a new captain,' Jean eventually informs us, 'an old and frail retired Chinaman. They left yesterday, but ran straight into rough weather. The captain became sick, and so they're back in port again.'

We're just absorbing this news when the children arrive with what is now becoming a familiar cry: 'A yacht! A yacht! It's Graham. He's in the pass.'

After coming ashore, Graham explains, 'We're really thankful to be here. We've had our troubles. It's taken us twenty days to sail the six hundred miles from Christmas Island to Caroline. To start with, the engine developed a problem, and then we've had nothing but light winds.'

Alve and John have left. The team has been joined by Anne's husband, Martin Garnett, who along with Kay is co-leader of the group. It's mostly for the benefit of Martin that they made such a big effort to return to Caroline.

'We weren't allowed to do any surveying of the other islands,' Graham says. 'The local government official on Christmas Island was in agreement with our plans, but the problem was with the main Kiribati government centre in Tawara.'

'They just wouldn't communicate,' Kay adds. She's very tired, and a large painful boil has developed on her leg. She's also angry because she has just seen another turtle in the Tahitians' fish trap.

It's not long before Adrien and his group arrive at the house. They take me aside. Adrien, as usual, is the spokesman. 'Ron,' he begins, 'would you ask the captain of *Te Manu* if he will take us back to Papeete with him?'

'We can cook them a feast of fresh turtle,' Gerald adds brightly.

First, I explain that a feast of fresh turtle would definitely not be appropriate (in fact it's illegal). I pass on the other request, to which Graham explains that with five aboard he is already overcrowded and still has his engine problems.

Jacob and Marere then become interested in Kay's boil. For at least an hour, they bathe it in hot water, then massage and squeeze her leg until with some jubilation the centre of the boil pops right out.

Alexandre is still following Graham everywhere he goes. They spend their time together searching for Graham's specialty: the bones of dead birds, as well as lizards, beetles, butterflies and shells.

Kay, on her first survey, found a small group of blue-grey noddies, but she has never been able to find their nest. Now Alexandre takes her by the hand and leads her far out onto the dry reef. There he shows her the small egg of the blue-grey noddy that rests peacefully in a recess of a large piece of coral. Later, in Kay's official report, six-year-old Alexandre has the honour and distinction of being recorded in the Smithsonian Institution of America as being the first person ever to find a blue-grey noddy's nest on Caroline Atoll.

Amid all this activity Jean again informs us that *Saturne* has left one more time. 'They should be all right this time,' he says, 'as they have aboard a crew member who understands the Sat-Nav and who was on their first two successful visits.'

The Tahitians' hopes are raised again. But they now have other troubles. Big swells from a storm far away to the west have been rolling in over the reef and the general water level around the lagoon and in the pass has risen markedly. Unfortunately, water has flowed over the top of their fish trap, and their six weeks of carefully collected fish have all escaped.

Saturne appears after three days, but there are no fish left to collect from the trap. The fishermen try trawling, but the now experienced sharks attack every last fish as it is hooked and devour it completely – including the plastic octopus lure. The fishermen quickly run out of lures and are obliged to return to Papeete with almost empty iceboxes. Not surprisingly, there are no volunteers to stay on the island.

Before leaving, they give us our shopping supplies, now much depleted by the continual pilfering of various crews while *Saturne* was making her three unsuccessful round trips.

The biologists are also ready to leave, and with fate again playing her mysterious hand, *Te Manu* and *Saturne* depart Caroline Atoll as they first arrived – at exactly the same moment.

For the next three months peace descends again. Left blissfully alone to our own occupations, we forget the outside world's pulls on Caroline for days at a time. The tourists have other destinations. The scientists stay at home to compile their reports. And the fishermen recuperate in port and count their losses. Although we enjoy these calm days and try not to think of the future, sometimes we feel as if we're just holding our breath anticipating the next invasion.

22

Paradise Lost

As September comes around once more, we prepare for our annual excursion and shopping trip to the outside world after a very disturbing year of incidents. The presence of the noisy parakeets is missed aboard but we have, by way of compensation, a female puppy from the union between Rocky and Kiki. We call her Lena, after Orama's daughter. She has Kiki's short legs and long back and the distinctive long nose of an Alsatian.

After an uneventful trip, we anchor once more in Cook's Bay, Moorea. Even though Moorea is relatively quiet compared to Papeete, and Caroline has recently been rather busy, it still takes us a little time to adjust to the constant noise and movement of people and machines as we look in towards the shore. Alexandre and Anaïs focus on the noisy yellow bulldozers and endless stream of cars that run along the road circling the bay. Jet skis buzz around the boat and helicopters continually disturb the air overhead. In the evening the lights that approach and fade away into the night keep the children up late in alert attention.

Next day we go ashore to collect our mail. We have a letter from Kay, who thanks us for our hospitality on Caroline and encloses a copy of a letter that she sent to the government of Kiribati describing Orama's illegal activities.

After detailing the killing of the turtles and general inter-ference with the wildlife, her letter finishes: 'We urgently request that your Ministry delay action on the final approval of Mr. Orama's lease.'

She tells us that with the support of OSTRAM (scien-tific research agency) in Tahiti, ICBP (birdlife protection) in Cambridge, England and TNCH (nature conservation) in Hawaii, she has made a proposal to turn Caroline Atoll into a world conservation zone with us as the caretakers. Kay's commitment is impressive. What I worry about is what repercussions this new attack on Orama will have, since he is not someone who takes criticism lightly.

After seeing to our shopping we head for Papeete to haul out the boat. In the harbour I run into Marere. He's sober, but excited as usual. He insists that we go and see Adrien. He takes us in his old jeep with no windscreen. He drives like a madman, screeching the tyres around corners, and has me thinking that negotiating Caroline's Blind Passage is not as recklessly dangerous as I had thought.

Adrien is polite but reserved. Lena does not greet me at all and appears to be angry about something. I'm now certain that they've been told about the activity of Kay Kepler and her letter to the Kiribati government. As we are mentioned in the letter, they must now assume that I'm working alongside the biologists to have their lease revoked.

'*Saturne* has been tied up in port for three months,' Adrien explains. 'We have some problems to clear up with the port authorities regarding the import of foreign fish, but once that's taken care of we plan to visit Caroline again.' He adds that two Kiribati government officials have recently met with Orama. They stayed at his hotel, where he wined and dined them for several days.

'Well,' I warn him, 'if you intend to return to Caroline, just make sure all your papers are in order before you leave;

otherwise, the biologists will find out that you're there illegally and may use this against you.'

He appears confused by my warning and offers to take me to meet Orama. I have no interest in becoming more involved in this continuing power struggle. My reason for going to Caroline was precisely to steer clear of this kind of conflict. Besides, I'm not yet ready to risk my life again in Marere's jeep, so I decline Adrien's offer of a lift and head back to the boat on foot.

The next day I take independent action, carefully typing out an official letter to the Kiribati Minister of the Phoenix and Line Islands, who lives on Christmas Island and is responsible for Caroline Atoll. I describe the recent activities of the biologists, the fishermen, and the surprise visit of *World Discoverer*. Then I explain how we acted as hosts to each group and how we are ideally placed to act as guardians of the island, answerable directly to the Kiribati government. I tell them about our transceiver capabilities and give the times and frequency of the coffee klatch radio schedules. I mention that we already have a radio friend on Christmas Island, Phil Wilder. To conclude, I say that we are not seeking any payment, but that we want only to be allowed to stay on Caroline. I add that we will remain totally responsible for our own health and welfare.

'You're dreaming,' Anne says. 'Orama has the Kiribati government in his back pocket. That's the way politics works in the Pacific islands. It's who you know that counts.'

'I don't agree,' I reply. 'The government has nothing to lose and everything to gain by making us guardians.'

'Dreamer,' she repeats. 'You'll see.'

I post my letter and we finish our shopping and health check-ups. Following the advice of the biologists, Omer's warnings, and in the interests of her love life, we leave our cat, Dou-Dou, with the people at the Biological Station on Moorea. We head back to Caroline with our menagerie reduced to only the two dogs, mother and daughter: Kiki and Lena.

We head once again away from the hard bustle of organised society towards the soft embrace of Caroline's arms. On arrival, the entrance to the pass, for once, is dead calm, and we can enter without the slightest difficulty. We slowly ease our way past the Tahitians' abandoned fish trap and quietly pick up our mooring. There is no turtle or friendly Napoleon to welcome us home.

'Getting in was too easy!' Anne comments. 'It's a bad omen.'

With a year's supply of goods aboard, ample bananas, papayas and vegetables, sixty hens and twenty ducks, we have no food worries. The bees are working for us, and there are always fish in the trap. The concrete tank is full of water. We should be sighing with relief at our good fortune, but we can't. What we don't have is an officially stamped piece of paper that says we can stay here on this isolated island in the home we have created with our own hands. That remains out of reach.

Not long after settling back on Ana-Ana, we have a caller on the coffee klatch net. He says he's on Christmas Island and is looking for Ron on Caroline Atoll. I pick up the call and we change to another frequency. He introduces himself as Tekinaiti Kaiteie, the Minister for the Phoenix and Line Islands. He talks slowly and seriously. 'I've received your application to be caretaker, Ron, and I've heard quite a lot about you and your family from the biologists who visited here this year. Caroline Atoll is my responsibility and, being so isolated, has always been a problem to administer. I am absolutely in favour of you acting as guardian and working directly for me.'

'It's the Kiribati Minister,' I shout excitedly to Anne. 'Come quick and listen.'

'I still need the approval of the Parliament in Tarawa,' he continues, 'but I can get that when I make a visit there in the near future.'

I'm so excited that I have trouble finding words. I do manage to thank him for taking the trouble to find me on the radio, give him all the days when I'm likely to be listening in case he has reason to contact me, then thank him one more time.

It's perfect: we can stay on as guardians, watch any possible developments by Orama and, if Kay should have any success with her plans, we can easily combine our government-approved presence here with any developments in her project. As the weeks pass, we have regular contacts with 'Tek'. He is pleased to become a regular contributor to the coffee klatch net, adding bits of information about developments on Christmas Island.

The children, sensing our lighter mood, have made up a new game in which one chases the other through the trees and across the beaches, shouting, 'Aaaargh! Here comes Orama! Aaaargh! Here comes Orama!' In fact, there is no sign of Orama. Tek tells us that his fishing lease has expired. 'I'll be very interested if he does arrive,' he says. He confirms that shortly he will be presenting my application to Parliament in Tarawa.

The months pass agreeably, marked by the waxing and waning of the moon. Christmas comes and a new year begins. Tek is absent from the radio. Near the end of January he reappears. He is more serious than usual and wants me to join him on another frequency. Anne senses something is wrong, as do I, and stays by the radio.

'I have a problem, Ron,' he begins. 'When I presented your application to the Kiribati government in Tarawa,

I was informed that Orama had already submitted a letter with a bad report about you to the Parliament. Among other things, he indicated that you were involved in illegal business on the island. He says he knew nothing about you being on the island before he got there and denies giving you any permission to stay there. He wants you off the island.'

'I'm in an awkward position,' he continues. 'I know Orama's temporary licence to fish outside the reef has expired, and I want you to stay on and report back to me any illegal activities Mr Orama may be involved with on the island. The problem is, with Mr Orama's bad report the authorities aren't sure who is in the right. I don't know at this moment what's going to happen.'

'Orama has used his connections with the government to get back at the biologists by trying to have us removed from the island,' I declare to Anne.

'I told you he has the government in his pocket,' she replies.

I finish with Tek in a state of confusion, then turn again to Anne. 'There's something not right here. Tek says Orama has no rights on Caroline, yet he has the power to block an application recommended by a Member of Parliament. Can you make sense of that?'

'You don't know what he told the government,' she says. 'Maybe he said you were drug-running or involved in other illegal activities.'

'Like running a nudist colony.' I smile – but I'm not happy.

In desperation, I use the radio to contact Kay, Graham and Omer Darr and ask them if they would please send references about my personal character, my ideals and my activities on Caroline directly to the Kiribati government, as well as any other information they think may help clarify our situation and combat Orama's bad report. Two months slip by, but the joy of our routine is overshadowed by our uncertainty about the future.

'A ship! A really big ship!' the children cry two days after April Fools' Day. It looks like one of the French military destroyers from the naval base in Papeete harbour. We watch a longboat from the ship come in through the pass and make its way across the lagoon. On the beach a French officer jumps ashore. He doesn't smile and won't make eye contact. This is obviously not a social visit. Two Micronesians are then helped ashore. One, in police uniform, stands back while the other steps forward, gives a wet handshake and says he is the Chief Immigration Officer for the Republic of Kiribati.

It's all unreal, like a scene from a film that will not have a happy ending. We invite everyone up to the comfort and shade of the house. The military men refuse, saying that they prefer to remain on the beach. Our two officials come up to the house and make themselves comfortable at the kitchen table. They make no attempt to search for evidence of the possible illegal activities mentioned by Orama. In fact, they ask no questions about what we're doing here. We have all taken the trouble to be respectably dressed just in case it's our reputation for nudity that has offended them. They both sit inert while we prepare coffee and serve them fresh coconut biscuits.

Despite the presence of the children and our attempt at a welcome, the Chief Immigration Officer remains uncommunicative and formal. He mumbles a long description of their tedious journey around the Pacific to arrive here. From Tarawa in the old Gilbert Islands, they flew to Fiji, from Fiji to New Zealand, from New Zealand to Rarotonga in the Cook Islands, and then on to Tahiti. They were stuck in Tahiti until they managed to hitch a lift on the French military ship that brought them here. From here they will go on to Hawaii, from Hawaii back to Fiji and then finally back home to Tarawa. I am impressed by their determination to pay us a visit regardless of the difficulties involved in circumnavigating the Pacific and the considerable expense.

In spite of my anxieties about the purpose of their visit, I amuse myself for a moment imagining again that we might make it onto the front pages of the world's press, this time as the cause of a major multinational confrontation involving the governments of the Republic of Kiribati and France and the residents of a tiny coral atoll. The story would explain how the French government freely gave the small Republic of Kiribati military aid in the form of a destroyer to enable them to complete the difficult task of removing one of its own citizens, accompanied by a radical Scotsman and two Polynesian-born children from a tiny desert island. This radical Scot would be charged with the crime of reducing himself and his family to the primitive state of animals. This kind of radical behaviour, they would claim, could set a bad example to the rest of the civilised world. The influence of this family, with the obvious success of their lifestyle exacerbated by their shameless nudity, could in fact undermine the efforts of all human beings in their struggle to become civilised, well-organised and well-dressed people.

After his coffee and numerous biscuits the police officer forgets his responsibilities and the seriousness of this historic confrontation. He smiles comfortably and jokes around with the children. He openly admires and praises our house and says that it's a rare pleasure to drink real coffee and eat real coconut biscuits. Up to this point, the uncommunicative Immigration Officer has given absolutely no indication of the purpose of their epic voyage.

After a very long silence the Immigration Officer slowly eases two sheets of paper out of his inside pocket. He looks away in embarrassment as he slides them across the table. They are official government legal papers and carry the stamp of the Kiribati Minister of Foreign Affairs.

The first paper declares: 'Ronald Charles Falconer is an undesirable immigrant and therefore a prohibited immigrant'.

The second paper orders: 'Ronald Charles Falconer, now a prohibited immigrant and unlawfully present in Kiribati, is to be removed from Kiribati within six days'. It adds that, in the meantime, he may be legally imprisoned.

I look straight at the Immigration Officer as the realisation that we are being evicted sinks in. He and his government have gone to great trouble and expense to confront an obviously happy family who have done nothing more harmful than try to turn a hopeful dream into reality far from the kind of sordid hypocrisy that lies manifest in these documents on our kitchen table.

'You can appeal,' he mumbles as he slides away from the table.

On the beach Anne tries once more to be pleasant to the French soldiers from her own native land. She has no more success than before, evidently because we have been defined as undesirables. The men, having completed their dastardly deed, now organise themselves quickly and push off from our small beach. Alexandre and Anaïs wave, but it is to their backs.

It's unbelievable. I want to try to appeal, and I search out Tek on the radio. For his own particular reasons he doesn't tune in anymore or, if he's listening, he doesn't answer my calls. I'm alone and isolated. I can think of no way to proceed. We've officially been evicted, but left alone on the island. I can't bring myself to voluntarily walk away from all we've created here for no reason that makes any sense to me. Three weeks of indecision slip by. All the social forces that

I hoped to escape from have followed us here, crushing all our simple ideals. I have the strong feeling that our short story is coming to an end. I didn't come here to worry day after day about a conflict that is based on lies. I have little interest in defending myself against false accusations. That is not why I came to Caroline.

We spend our time discussing alternatives for our future. A family who own an isolated island in the Gambier Islands, and who regularly communicate with us by radio, have offered to share their island with us. We could also return to Ahe. For myself I am inclined to give adventuring a rest for a while and concentrate on my music, perhaps on the island of Moorea. We are right in the middle of planning our future when *Saturne* arrives.

'There's another boat behind,' Alexandre says quickly. I recognise Orama's other, larger, converted tugboat *Orio*. The two boats move up and down the reef behind Ana-Ana like gunboats on patrol.

'Why the show of strength?' I ask Anne, wondering what Orama is capable of.

It's the morning of our coffee klatch. I pick up Les on the radio.

'We're just a little afraid, Les. I'm sure they didn't expect us still to be here. They must be surprised and don't know what to do. They're not fishing, and I have no idea what they may do.'

Les informs us that he has heard through the grapevine that a Kiribati inter-island ship is preparing to leave Christmas Island for a visit to Caroline. 'They have police and officials aboard,' he adds. This throws another light on Orama's presence. Perhaps he's here for a rendezvous with the Kiribati officials.

The hours pass and Orama's boats rest silently behind Ana-Ana. No one comes ashore and there is no movement aboard. Eventually, Anne leaves for the fish trap with the children and dogs. I prepare a batch of dough with today's headline in mind: 'Invasion'.

Absorbed in the task of controlling the fire and oven, I start when I hear a movement in the trees. Two men emerge and approach the house. I recognise Orama, even though he's without his business suit, gold chains and brief-case. He's wearing light shorts, a T-shirt and plastic sandals. Without shaking hands with me, he introduces the captain of the *Orio*. I invite them to sit at our large table outside in the shade, where we face each other in silence. A powwow between the big warring chiefs.

'I'm surprised you're still here,' Orama starts, very calm, very polite. But soon the conversation deteriorates. I stand up, put my hands on the table in front of him, stare him straight in the face and shout: 'It's you who shit me! You told lies about us! It's because of you we have problems.'

The captain moves uncomfortably in the face of my fury, but Orama remains undisturbed. Perhaps he hasn't fully comprehended what I just blurted out in bad French, and I realise to my regret that I know no French words strong enough to express my rage. 'Wicked! wicked!' I translate, as if he were only a naughty child. 'You told lies to the govern-ment.' There are tears in my eyes as weeks of tension and frustration pour out. I struggle for suitable words to reveal my feelings, but I am limited to repeating simply 'Méchant! Méchant!'

Orama remains absolutely unmoved. I'm wasting my energy. I sit down calmly.

'Sometimes,' he begins, taking his time in the manner of a smooth-talking politician, 'it's necessary to do certain things. I have an international group working against me. I've seen their letters. Your name is included.'

I begin slowly to explain my priorities to Orama, telling

him that all I want to do is remain here on the island. I remind him of all the help I gave him and his workers when they were marooned here.

'You warned Adrien not to come here,' he declares. 'My men are afraid of you – that's why I had to come here myself, my men are too afraid to come here.'

'I told Adrien simply as a friend that, if they were planning to come back to Caroline, they should be sure that all their papers were in order, otherwise the biologists would use any illegal voyage against you. I don't have the power to stop people coming here. I was just simply giving him helpful, friendly advice.'

But I have lost Orama's attention. I concentrate on the captain, who has been more attentive. 'I have done nothing against Orama, the biologists or the government,' I tell him. 'In fact, I've helped everybody who came here to the best of my ability. Now, as a result, I'm being evicted, and all because of some lies Orama has told to the government.' The captain, at least, appears to accept my explanation. He begins a long discussion with Orama in Tahitian. Eventually, Orama sits back on his bench. He pauses dramatically.

'Perhaps I've been mistaken,' he says, with an expression that implies that, at least from his point of view, all has been forgiven. 'All you have to do now is leave for a few months. Then, you can come back and act as guardian for me,' he adds, pleased to have provided a solution to all our problems.

I'm just beginning to adjust to this change of tactics when Anne arrives. She recognises Orama immediately despite his island attire. I wait in suspense for the tigress that I know rests inside her to emerge. She moves intensely and aggressively towards Orama, then freezes. She remains there almost touching his nose. She has no problem finding the right French words to damn him to hell and back as she screams and spits directly into his face.

I don't intervene; Orama deserves even more. The captain is again uncomfortable but doesn't interfere either. Orama just about manages to keep control, but his face displays a solid grimace that makes him look like he's actually smiling. After Anne's stream of invective eventually runs dry, I take the opportunity to explain to her that, in fact, we have reached a slightly better understanding. Since everyone has now had their say, the powwow is over. Orama and the captain leave to return to their boat.

The next day, Orama arrives early on Ana-Ana. He comes with a warm smile and two fresh black jack fish. We sit for a moment on the coral, nervous but prepared to give our new understanding a chance. I tell him about the Kiribati inter-island boat that is coming.

'When exactly will it arrive?' he asks a little too quickly.

'In three or four days' time,' I reply, watching his pensive reaction to this new information.

'Mr Orama,' I continue, 'I think we now agree that we have no real conflict of interest here on Caroline. If we meet together with the Kiribati officials who are coming, perhaps it may be possible to save my situation.'

He looks the other way, then says, 'We won't be here in three days' time.'

'Well, leave me a letter confirming your position,' I say, but he is not listening. We sit another long moment in silence.

'What about the treasure of Caroline?' he says eventually.

For a moment I'm stunned. He's not here to meet the government officials, and since his fishing licence hasn't been renewed, he is not here to fish either. Did he really come up here personally to hunt for hidden treasure? The question of lost treasure on Caroline has never entered my mind.

'Or maybe you have already found it,' he adds, looking

straight at me to verify the truth of whatever I might reply.

I smile as I think to myself, yes, I've found treasure here – but not anything like what Orama is looking for. I hope my enigmatic expression causes Orama to wonder if I may indeed have found his kind of treasure.

'Try Nake Islet,' I suggest. 'Over a hundred years ago J. T. Arundel, who was then head of the New Zealand Company's settlement here, began to demolish the sacred marae, looking for treasure. He completely destroyed one wall. Halfway through the second, bigger wall, he stopped. Why? Did he find the treasure, or did the sacred forces drive him away before he found it?'

Orama is listening intently. He excuses himself to join his crew on the beach. They leave immediately in their speedboat for Nake Islet.

The rest of the day is calm and uneventful. The two tugs remain in place behind Ana-Ana. By nightfall the speed-boat has not returned. We're ready for bed when a tired Orama appears on the path. He explains that a combination of low water and the maze of coral throughout the lagoon caused them a lot of trouble and held them up.

'Have you a flashlight I can borrow?' he asks politely. They plan to head out to sea by way of Blind Passage, then make their way all around South Islet to arrive back at their boat on the lee side.

I give him my best flashlight. After he leaves I make my way out onto the beach, where I sit quietly on the high coral to watch their boat successfully exit the pass into the open sea. I continue my watch until, after a long time, I see them reappear from around South Islet and climb back aboard their boat. Knowing that everyone is in their place, I retire to bed.

In the morning a sailor returns with the flashlight. 'We're leaving for Nake Islet,' is all he says.

The tugs leave their familiar place behind Ana-Ana. For two days we watch them far to the north, hanging around Nake Islet. Then they disappear. Orama has gone and we are left alone on the island to face the fate he has set in motion.

23

The End of an Adventure

The Kiribati ship, we're informed, is on its way. We now have to make a decision. I'm tempted for a moment to brave it out with the government officials.

'What can they do?' I ask Anne. 'We've done absolutely nothing wrong.'

'Well, they're not just going to give you another warning and sail away once more. You'll be arrested and put in prison on board if necessary. We'll all be taken back to Christmas Island. They'll burn the houses and kill all the hens and ducks, and you'll lose *Fleur d'Ecosse* because they'll just leave her here.'

'They can't do that,' I declare. 'We're not wanted criminals.'

'They would simply be obeying orders from their democratically elected government,' she says. 'You can't fight against that.'

'I'm tempted to try,' I say. 'I want to tell the true story.'

'And the children?' she says. 'A drama like that would destroy all the peace and security they've enjoyed here. And for us, too – we've been beaten by underhanded politics, that's all. They can never take away all the years of pleasure and fun we've had here. So long as we still have the boat and our belongings we're free and independent.'

I think about this for a while. If we found enough exposure to tell our story, people would soon realise the truth. Maybe then we could come back to the island. However, I have no wish to become the victim of someone's perverse personality as a captive animal. I don't want the climax of my personal dream to take place in a prison cell.

There is no right and wrong in my head, though – only people doing their own thing. We all have dreams. Maybe my dream has served its purpose and it is now time to move on. We can remain independent, free to indulge in any other adventure that comes our way. We can leave at a time when we have everything. This experience will rest forever in our minds as something that finished on a high, never having had the time to perhaps dwindle into mediocrity. We will remember that during our time here we appreciated every last moment of every day as a very special and precious gift.

'Okay, okay, maybe you're right,' I say to Anne. 'It would be a real mess. It's hard to face, but it looks like we have to leave.' Once I say the words, the inevitability of it all surges through my body in a deflating wave of sadness.

With only one day left, we have to pack up all our belongings, load up the boat and exit the pass. We've collected so much stuff over the years that we are obliged to select only the most important things to take with us. Alexandre and Anaïs hold on to their most precious toys, while Anne and I sort out what we have to leave behind.

We pack up the radio, most of the food and the things that are essential to the boat. We take almost all our personal items. Anne leaves some of her books but takes her best shells and the three small glass fishing balls she found on arrival. I take my woodworking tools, the solar panels and the wheat grinder. What we leave behind are the garden tools, heavy-duty batteries, a defunct all-band radio receiver, mattresses, all kinds of pots and pans as well as the bees and bee gear. Once started, our packing is a fast and concentrated effort with little time for sentiment and reflection. Kiki and Lena sulk around, sensing the change.

Mini-Mini is now loaded for the last time. Anne and the children are on the beach. Alone, I take a slow look around our settlement and all we are leaving – the house, kitchen and cookhouse, the garden that we worked so hard for and, sadly, our hens and ducks. Tears flow down my cheeks as I look back on our time here as a small complete family involved in a very special adventure.

Yes, I found treasure here on Caroline: an understanding of the fundamental source of power that creates everything, a humility about my own tiny place in the immense and unknown universe, a sense of being at one with the world, the ability to accept myself and everything else for what it is, and the courage to keep on trying.

Finally we – sharing the fate of so many other people and animals in the world today – have been forced to move on by commercial exploitation and greed. For us, though, it is not the end of the road as it was for the American Indians, Australian Aborigines and the tribes of the Amazon, and still could easily be for the Pacific Polynesians. We remain independent and flexible, able to travel on as easily as the migrating birds. We are nomads free as the wind, travelling minstrels, with our boat for transport to take us where we please.

We are not defeated. We are simply moving on. We will thoughtfully choose our next port of call, be it another island adventure or other style of life. No matter where our paths take us, we have shared our moment, together alone, on Caroline Atoll.

Epilogue

Alongside the ants of Ana-Ana, we played out our time occupied in the simple task of establishing a place to raise our children and fend off invaders. Our invaders won, as invaders often do.

We did try settling on another remote island, sharing our lives with the family already installed there. The island bulldozer cleared a site for us high on the side of the volcanic mountain. We built a house from modern materials and raised an impressive garden in the rich volcanic soil. But after isolation, sharing wasn't easy and conflicts of ideals were a constant irritation. Then a full cyclone passed directly over the island, picking up our new house and fragile dreams and depositing them like matchwood in the jungle.

Disillusioned and unsettled, we moved back to Moorea. Caroline had been the climax of our adventuring; there was nothing more. Spent and ready for a total change, we rented a house and bought a car. I hadn't driven in ten years.

Anne had difficulties compromising her freedom in a new teaching job. I approached the local restaurants and hotels with my autoharp and harmonica act. Since they seemed supportive, I bought an amplifier and put together a program of good old songs. I played in the dining rooms, they paid me, and they asked me back.

Alexandre and Anaïs became the only Europeans in an all-Polynesian school, where they encountered stealing and lying for the first time. Once initiated into the system of civilised society, they did well with their lessons. Anaïs became quite upset if she didn't hold first place in her class, while Alexandre, the distracted dreamer, stayed respectably in the top five. Both children had a problem initially with certain infections, since they had never had to build up an immunity.

Orama's fishing lease was never renewed.

When the government of the new Pacific nation of Kiribati decided to place all its islands in the same time zone it arbitrarily moved the International Date Line 2000 miles eastward to include its farthest-flung landfall, Caroline Island. Renamed Millennium Island, the site of this book became the first place on earth to witness the dawning of the year 2000.

For the New Year 2000 celebrations, a considerable group of Kiribati islanders, along with a television team, installed themselves temporarily on Caroline. When the millennium television coverage began, the whole world watched what up until then had been our personal morning gift, the first new rays of the sun. Tiny Caroline, the first land on our planet to welcome in the new century, was to become famous overnight and to be blessed as a symbol of hope.

Kay Kepler and the Prime Minister of Kiribati were on the island for the celebrations. Kay wrote me later to say that she had established good relations with the new Prime Minister and that her plans for creating a nature reserve on Caroline were looking very positive.

At this time, Caroline remains uninhabited and peacefully alone.

Conversion table

Polynesia is a mix of metric and imperial systems of measurement. Likewise, Ron uses both. Please refer to the conversion table for clarification.

Length, distance and area	Multiply by
Inches to centimetres	2.54
Centimetres to inches	0.39
Feet to metres	0.30
Metres to feet	3.28
Yards to metres	0.91
Metres to yards	1.09
Miles to kilometres	1.61
Kilometres to miles	0.62

Weight	
Ounces to grams	28.35
Grams to ounces	0.035
Pounds to kilograms	0.45
Kilograms to pounds	2.21

Temperature
To convert C to F multiply by 1.8 and add 32
To convert F to C subtract 32 and divide by 1.8

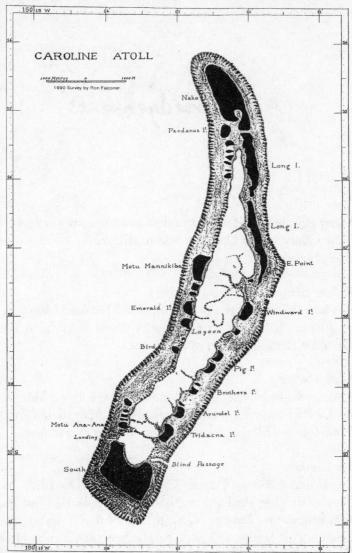

CAROLINE ATOLL

1000 Metres · 1000 M
1990 Survey by Ron Falconer

Nake
Pandanus I.
Long I.
Long I.
E. Point
Motu Mannikiba
Emerald I.
Windward I.
Lagoon
Bird
Pig I.
Brothers I.
Arundel I.
Motu Ana-Ana
Landing
Tridacna I.
South
Blind Passage

This is the most accurate chart that exists for Caroline Atoll. It was reoriented with the aid of position points taken by Dr Graham Wragg's GPS Sat.Nav. and redrawn using aerial photographs supplied by a New Zealand survey plane and donated by Kay Kepler.

Acknowledgements

Many people contributed in one way or the another to our final adventure on Caroline and to this story. I will always cherish your help.

For the circumnavigation
Sue MacIntosh; Neake Skeats on *Wylo*; Bernard Moitessier on *Joshua*; Tom Neale on Suvarov; Carol Dunlop in Fiji; Caroline Reese-Davis from Australia.

In the Pacific
Ronnie, for being there; anonymous yachtee in the Marquesas for Kwili; Graham Neelson for Raki; Arii, Mama Fana, Papa Toa and all the population of Ahe for everything.

For Caroline
David and Criss on *Persuit*; Captain Omer Darr; Les and Gloria Whitley; Paul and Sophia on *Denebola*; Bernard and Véronique on *Tamata*; George on *Sheila*; Olivier and Lawrence on *Iferouane*; Joseph for the bees; Kay Kepler PhD; Captain Graham Wragg on *Te-manu*; Anne and Martin Garnett; Marke, John and Alve; Adrien, Jacob, Marere, Gerald.

On boats and yachts
Conrad and crew on *Royal Dawn*; Margarete Hicks; Luke
and Jan on *Cynus*; Jo, Ken and Aileen on *Shanakie*; Piere
and Robert on *Sauvage*; Wally, Susan, young Wally and
Debbie on *Fortune*; Emmet on *Kamahele*; Humphrey and
Clair on *Drumby*; Claude and Russ on *Quetzal*; Frederic
on *Hippocrate*; Brian and Roy on *Finesse*; Peter and Per on
Sheila; Sergio and Maria Cristena on *Bio*; Jesus, Monica,
Severine and little Chiloe on *Amanita*; Wilfred, Pascal,
Colin and Arthur on *Kalabush*; John Luke and Christine
on *Boris*; Bengt Danielson, Marie Therese, and Edmundo on
World Discoverer.

Regular radio friends
Les (Moorea); Little Earl (Tahiti); Fred (Hawaii); Bill
(Hawaii); Arnold (Rarotonga); Phil (Christmas Island);
Miralda (Pitcairn Island); Ron (Marshall Islands); Bill and
Georgina (Raiatea); Browny (Hawaii); Perry (Fanning
Island); Dr John (New Zealand); Des (Aitutaki Island);
Helmut (Moorea); Anne (Moorea); Nancy on the *Edna*;
Michael on *Solan Goose*; P.P.E Bill (Chicago); Criss (New
Zealand); Jean (Tahiti); Tihoni (Kamaka Island); Tex
(Luisianna).

And for the book
Peter Kittel; Jan Prince; Greig La Shelle; Alex Du Prel;
Lies Claris-Lafourcade; Phillippe and Michelle Perrolaz de
Boissieu; Stanley Falconer; Don and Mary Decker; Murray
Ashton; Natasha Fairweather; Kristen Amundsen; Kay
Kepler PhD; Dr Graham Wragg; Jane Herman; Harriet
Allen; Elana McCauley; Jo Jarrah; Nadine Davidoff; Jude
McGee.